Sweetly Be!

Rose Budd Stevens

*With Rose Budd's Glossary
of Old-Timey Expressions*

A Muscadine Book
University Press of Mississippi
Jackson and London

Text pages designed by Ruth Williams; section pages designed by Rand
Williams and Cindy Warfield-Clark.

Library of Congress Cataloging-in-Publication Data

Stevens, Rose Budd.
    Sweetly be! / by Rose Budd Stevens ; with Rose Budd's glossary
of old-time expressions.
        p. cm.
    "A Muscadine book."
    ISBN 0-87805-465-0
    1. Country life—Southern States. 2. Southern States—Social life
and customs—1865— I. Title.
F216.2.S74   1990   90-43224
975-dc20   CIP

Contents

Folks and Tales

Daily Parades and Other Adventures on the Farm

Preface

When I began writing my first newspaper column I had no idea I would be writing forty-three years later. Over the years loyal readers have clipped and saved columns they liked, and written to me about the ones they didn't agree with. Readers have named their children Rose Budd for me, Dale for my husband, Joe, Tim, and Rose, Jr., for our sons and daughter.

When this book was in the talking stage I asked readers to send their favorite columns to me. They did and many of them appear in this book. One reader said, "Mama loved reading about Jimson Yarber and longed to meet him. Will you include the enclosed clipping in your new book *Sweetly Be!* in honor of her?" This column I have included along with many others sent as favorites. In fact this book is made up of readers' selections. I know you will also love Mary Martha Twilberry and her rememberings of times after 1842, the year she was born, as she recalls a man named Williams Paul.

I invite you to read my other two books, *Along the R.F.D. with Rose Budd Stevens* and *From Rose Budd's Kitchen*, a cookbook that reads like a story book and has lots of ideas for good cooking, too.

If you travel Highway 24 west of McComb, Mississippi, I ask you to watch for a yellow ribbon tied on an oak tree beside our driveway (directly across from a red brick church). We will have a cup of tea, and I will show you our many saved and well-loved things that we used to keep family and home together back in the days of the Depression.

Sweetly be,
Rose Budd Stevens

Stories from
Before My Time

Who Was
Williams Paul?

M ary Martha Twilberry speaks throughout the story as it was
told to me years ago.

"Yes, it seems to me that when Williams Paul came, it was getting on toward hot summer or mayhap it is my memory failing me
and it was an early spring. Early violets were blooming down in
the vales and by little streams before frost quit visiting on the hills
and turning everything black with its icy fingers. Or could be that
a cold spell came in early summer, for I recollect a time in June when
snow fell and things seemed turned upside for a while. Things seem
so dim to me now. I recall many summers and the Big Book shows
marked plain as anything 1842 as my birthdate.

"You see, we once didn't have a Bible and Pa got tired of borrowing cousin Sile's. Pa ordered off and got our own Great Book.
When it came, Ma blew on the conch shell. Pa came running, for
she never bothered him in the fields unless something special happened or it was meal time. The same man who took the order brought
the Book; I well recall his trap buggy, a frail thing of two wheels,
hardly big enough to hold the doughty Mr. Sells.

"I recollect his horse as plain as if it was yesterday—big splayed
feet from traveling over hill and dale from where we lived to Louisiana and some said on down to the Gulf of Mexico, and a long
flowing mane, creamy white, ripply and wavy. I wished my hair was
like the mane in place of the many tight curls that covered my head
like a fur cap. I disremember the color of the horse but do know
its teeth were bad. Mr. Sells was kind and cooked up a mess of meal
and milk sweetened with brown sugar from a tote bag hanging under
the middle of the trap buggy.

"When Pa came running to the house, Mr. Sells had the Bible
out and his goose quill resharpened for putting down the days of
birthing of the nine children still living. Pa couldn't write his name
and wouldn't know it if he saw it wrote down; he had to take Ma's
word for it. Ma could read a few words and could only print on
wide lines if a copy had been set for her. Mr. Sells wrote my name
with a fancy flourish, scrolls and frills. He showed me where he

spelled my name, Mary Martha Twilberry. The *T* did wind and twine about itself.

"Ma could remember the living ones' birthdays, but she needed help in bringing to mind the comings and goings of the little ones who rested under the sod in the lower part of the graveyard, the part below the picket fence. That is, all but Little Flower, who was laid by the side of young Sarah from the big house. You see, they played together and took ill at the same time. Smallpox it was; many died from this bad thing that came out of the blue, it seemed. All these scars on my face came from smallpox.

"Me rambling and not telling about the Paul man! Goodness, that is what you came down here for to hear about—Williams Paul, who came wandering to our place with nothing to his name but a fancy comb in a blue case, a well polished buckeye, a pair of brass-toed shoes in a hide bag. He was barefooted and his feet were red and chapped from the cold ground. His clothes were tattered and held together with patches which Ma said needed to be patched, too. His eyes were the bluest I had ever seen and teeth so white they seemed to be made of bleached bones. You recall the bones of dragged-off cows after nature has disposed of the flesh and when sun and rain take over bleaching the bones white as snow? Just so were his teeth.

"He had a kind heart and a pair of willing hands and the name of Williams Paul. Master was willing to put him up for a few months in return for some carving to be done on a set of dining room chairs and the big table too. Seems how the family got so used to him being around to tell tales of the places he had been, but to hear him tell, none so fair and restful as the farm on Waggoner Creek in Amite County. He stayed and made his home in the shed room where the old grandmother had lived until smallpox took her.

"Oh! He had a loving heart. Many is the night when I would be on the porch in the heat, fanning a little smudge in an old cracked black iron pot so the smoke would keep the night insects away. I would see him, torch in hand, going to tend a cow about to calve or climbing a tall tree to put a hapless baby bird back in the nest so the prowling tom cats couldn't feast of its plump breast. His was a tender heart; he kept the small children entertained by the hour, so Mistress wouldn't switch their fat legs until red streaks made a checkerboard thereon.

"He could make the biggest 'sugar-teats' in a flash, and did I relish one if it was my day to tend the handicapped child in the family. I declare I hadn't thought of Tippy in nigh eighty years till this very minute—Tippy with pipe stem legs, long slender hands, teeth sharp as a kitten's, and how he would bite a piece out of you if things didn't go his way. His head was as big as the cedar water bucket on the back porch wash shelf. How do I know? Once we heard a visitor snigger about Tippy being a waterhead child. When the bucket was empty, I turned it over his head and it fit. Even if he couldn't talk we knew what he wanted by his grunts and motions. Little Tippy, how he loved cold fresh water either to drink or play in.

"Williams Paul made the cutest little frame to fit around Tippy's neck to hold up his head. Mistress padded it with cloth soft as down under the wings of wild ducks. It was strapped to his shoulders. Many were the times when it was real hot and we had Tippy down at the branch playing, and we would unbuckle the frame and slip it off so the cool breeze could fan his little neck, so soft and white. How I loved to curl his little duck tails over my fingers and make them stand out in a ruff around his head.

"He was a good, patient child, holding his head with both hands to keep it from wobbling while we tried on and wore his frame. His eyes were dark brown, the color of a muscadine left in the sun too long, and he had the longest lashes you ever saw. I recall Mistress saying his lashes should have belonged to Roseena who was pretty except for her stubby lashes. (I recall she wore a dried toad frog in a little sack around her neck for months, only it didn't do a bit of good. Never again did she believe in one of her grandma's cures, since no long lashes grew.)

"Many is the day Tippy drank fifteen cups of water, greedy and holding the cup with both hands. He had a special cup, blue speckled granite with a big handle easier for him to hold that his papa brought from Natchez when he walked there for medicine for his aged mama.

"What happened to Tippy? I disremember at the moment, seems like he went away on a trip. No, no, wait a moment. Mistress set the older house children to tending Tippy one day while I was helping strip red oak bark to make dye for a batch of wool already spun to thread. We had already dyed hanks and hanks of blue thread from indigo Mr. Wash had raised on that special patch across the creek; it wouldn't grow nowhere else but in that one. (Brown dye was easy to come by for we gathered walnut hulls by the basket and stored them in the old sheep shed.)

"The children from the house and many of my brothers and sisters decided to give Tippy a ride in the goat cart. This was without Mistress knowing about it—she was careful of Tippy as could be. Her old-age baby, she called him. She loved him even if he was large of head and humped of back. He was getting on in age, must have been ten or twelve years old. He 'twarnt much bigger than a small five-year-old except for his head.

"Well, the children hitched the goats, five of them—two behind, two in front, and the lead goat, a great big billy goat with long chin whiskers, yellow eyes and wide polished horns. I never trusted that billy and would never have allowed him to be lead goat if I hadn't been off stripping red oak bark. They said Tippy was happy riding in the cart and knowing he would get to put his feet in the wet weather branch at the foot of a hill. As they went up a little hill the lead goat was stung by ground hornets and ran away leading the four goats to follow. The cart hit a sand rock and turned over, throwing Tippy out of the cart to strike his head on another rock, killing him at once.

"I was coming through a thicket when I heard all this commotion and moaning. When I reached the accident, Mr. Paul had Tippy in his arms, taking him to his mama. Mistress went into a swoon, began to have a crying fit, and carried on until Sallie brought out the ball of opium gum and cut off a piece for Mistress to chew, which calmed her down.

"I don't remember where Tippy was buried—I think in the part of the graveyard that fell in the branch years ago. I recall a few bones scattered about long after the last one of the family died. There never was a gravestone to Tippy's grave; a solid pine-heart board was driven at the head of the piled-up mound with a picture of Tippy carved in the wood by Mr. Paul.

"Mr. Williams Paul—how my mind wanders—seems only yesterday when he came to the farm. He stayed a long time, seems like it was during high waters in the spring time. I recall how the creek was out of its banks, kneading the bluff below the blue hole with dark muddy fingers that slowly pulled bits of the bank with each surge and rush. Big trees went tumbling by, and once we saw a mama 'possum with five little ones holding on to her tail floating by on a tree. I remember my brothers Scooner and Booger wishing they could get their hands on the mama and babies, then put them in a pen to fatten to eat all at one meal.

"When wild pecans ripened along with black walnuts and hickory nuts, Scooner and Booger would spend days wandering and gathering the nuts, and they wouldn't share! They knew where pawpaws grew in a big thicket. They ate their fill several times a day and grew fat and shiny. Maypops and mulberries were treats for those two, who ate everything without washing, bugs and all, I reckon. They roamed the pastures, milking a cow when they were hungry, drinking the milk hot and foamy from a big old cooter shell they carried along for that very reason.

"That Scooner was a sight! He died a long time ago. A snake bit him and he swelled up twice his size, suffering for five days in such pain he bit his own arm until blood ran on the floor. Master wanted Ma and Pa to let him and a neighbor smother Scooner between two feather beds like they had done for a great aunt who went mad after a mad dog bit her. Ma and Pa had great faith in a snake or mad stone they had come by in past years, only it didn't work. Seems like my people had great faith in these certain stones called healing stones. You have to watch real close when bad stormy weather comes and there are flashes of lightning. When a bolt strikes a tree, if a person can get to the tree quick and dig at the roots where the bolt entered the ground, there will be a stone— sometimes a sort of flat stone, but most of the time a round rough ball kind. Lucky the person who gets there before the stones have vanished.

"The next day, in respect for Scooner, Mama dressed us in our best clothes, faded but clean. We went through the pine forest to the back side of the upper place to the graveyard. When we got near the grave, we could hear this raspy rattle sound like dried peas in a gourd. Pa was ahead bending down briars and weeds for the little children. I heard him cry out, "Go back, go back." Mama stopped the small children. I scooted to the side and got a full view of Scooner's grave. Right in the middle was the biggest rattlesnake, coiled in a heap with head high and tail rattling for fair.

"For years the story of the mate to the snake that bit our brother was told around low-burning fires and in the cotton fields. Of course, they had buried Scooner at night. Anybody knows a person who has such a death from a rattlesnake bite, if buried in day time, will cause them doing the burying to have to fight off the other snakes trying to avenge the one that was killed. The snake that bit our brother was a big one—twelve rattles and lots of buttons. My pa stretched the skin on a board and made a belt from it.

"My mind wanders, and I get off the story of Williams Paul. Now I think it was either a hot spring or early summer when he came, for the crows were sitting in trees waiting for the planted corn to sprout so they could steal the corn. I recall lots of children being in the fields to scare the crows away. How we played up and down the rows!

"I remember the birds had set and some had hatched; I recall four French mockingbirds in a tall sycamore tree near the wet bog, down by the old slough where we crossed to go visit Aunt Symathrias with a hoecake wrapped in a woolen scarf. She was a widow with no children, and her kin had to help her out. Those same four mockingbirds sat and waited for their mama to bring them mulberries trip after trip. I made markings in the dirt to see how many berries the one on the end ate; it was as many as I had fingers on both hands, so it must have been spring.

"I remember one Fourth of July when Mr. Paul decided to give all on the place a good loud day. Somewhere he got hold of a bucket of black gunpowder and talked Master into letting him take the anvil from its place on a hewed hickory log waist high on thick sturdy legs. You see, plow points and even logging chains were beat out on the anvil. We stood around to watch Mr. Paul dig a deep hole way down in the pasture, near the sheep shed, and also a long trench to the hole. Next he filled the hole with the gunpowder and put a nice stream of powder in the trench. It took the tenants, Jed and Cynrus, and two visitors from below Jawbone Creek to place the anvil over the powder-filled hole. All stood back well out of harm's way, because once the powder was lit, there was no way of telling which way the anvil would go and where it would land.

"Way down near Agnes Branch a big trench had been dug and two sheep had been cooking over the coals all night. This was to be our treat for our hard work so far this year. The loud bang came, and the anvil rose and flew through the air toward Agnes Branch. It landed right in the middle of the roasting sheep. Ashes, meat, and burning sticks went up and came down everywhere. We picked through the wreck, finding tasty bits of meat to eat with corn cakes."

On one of my visits to Mary Martha I asked her what became of Booger. "Well," she said, "now let me see. He was giving my folks so much trouble wanting to go to Hog Eye play parties and staying out until dusk dark. Those folks in the Hog Eye community was a rough lot; they always had a still going and sometimes drank too much of what they stilled. Pa decided to send Booger over to Liberty to live with a man who owned a tanyard right on Speculation Creek. There Booger was taught to tan hides and make shoes and saddles. He learned to weave girthings and bridle reins. He would go to Natchez, which was sixty miles away, by ox wagon to help bring back lime and casts of oil used in the tanning of hides. Booger thought he was grown when he drove the oxen half a day.

"You wonder how a stilling of whiskey was made back when I was a young girl. Bring me my Bible from under my bed and I'll see if there is a recipe for a small stilling. I remember Mr. Williams Paul had such a 'set-up' at the backside of the old field below the blue hole on Waggoner Creek. 'Twas many a demijohn of the spirits stored in a cave to be doled out to a favorite few. I would take pleasure if you would read me the words put down when my pa and ma were living."

A Receipt for Stilling

In a tub that holds 13 bushels, put in 12 half-bushels of boiling water and one bushel and a half of corn meal. STIR IT WELL. Take one gallon of rye meal and sprinkle over top, put one gallon of malt on that, let stand 48 hours, then add two half bushels of cold water, stir four or five times in two hours, then it will begin to work. Then carefully measure 20 gallons of cold spring water and add. When cooked off proper, you will not fail to make five gallons of good whiskey.

The paper was tattered and torn, and there were no directions for stilling off to make whiskey. Mary Martha seemed to think everyone knew how to tend a still. She continued:

"I want to tell you about the year it was so cold we nearly froze to death and would have if our pa hadn't been a good manager, keeping plenty of liderd knots and firewood on hand. The ponds and creeks froze solid, and ice had to be melted in wash pots so the livestock could drink. That winter was awful! We had warm clothes made from wool clipped from sheep right here on the place.

The cold was like nothing even the old folks had seen before. You could sit right in front of the open fire, and water would freeze beside you. Ma put thick layers of straw and hay on the floor and laid down two old carpets over them to keep out the seeping bitter cold. The little children slept spoon-fashion, four to a bed pallet. Pa stayed up all night keeping the fire going, and Ma baked sweet potatoes in the ashes for our breakfast.

"The creeks froze solid, and we slipped and slid trying to skate. Kate from the big house had a pair of things she strapped to her feet. She could flash along the ice on thin sharp blades on the bottom of laced-up shoes. Once she skated all the way to where the old beech log used to be at the bend of the creek. It was nearly dark when she got home. Master raised Cain and she wasn't to go out of the house for two weeks. We didn't mind—you see, I stayed with her for company. Her mama wouldn't hear of having her cooped up with only younger children to play with. We had a fireplace in her room and a good feather bed to sleep in, and we sunk so deep in it and were covered so well the cold didn't bother us one bit. My pay for the week? Master bought me my first pair of new shoes from the tanyard shop on Speculation Creek where the shoes were made. These were called pegged shoes and were so stiff I just lumbered along until they got broke in.

"The chickens and other fowl were sights. Their combs and wattles froze and fell off, and some had frozen feet and had to be killed. You have heard the old saying, 'Cold enough to freeze the horns off a billy goat'? Well, that happened! Every billy goat and every ram sheep had frozen horns that dropped off. Even the oxen left out in the weather had frozen horns. No more did they click and clack their horns against each other when pulling the big sleds.

"We found dead birds everywhere. It was so cold they would be flying and freeze right in the sky, dropping in droves. Down on the creek, ducks froze in the ice, dying before the thaw came. I recall Master saying, 'The bugs will ruin us next year.' (Sure enough the gardens and fields were riddled by bugs, for there were no birds to eat them. Only the martins came as usual to the hanging gourds to swoop about making pretty designs in the sky.)

"The cave below the mill tail was filled with slabs of ice, the opening filled with sawdust from the water sawmill, and a thick facing of boards put in place. How we enjoyed cold shrubs and wines using this ice in hot summertime.

"Williams Paul died in that cold time. The ground was too frozen to dig a grave, and it was too cold for folks about to come to a wake. Mistress came up with the idea of building a log fire where the grave would be dug. This was done, and the children wanted to help. I recall taking armfuls of frozen limbs to throw on the low-burning logs. We begged sweet potatoes from the potato banks to cook in the coals and peanuts to parch in the edges of the coals. Mistress didn't allow that, said it wasn't fitting.

"There was a right nice turnout. People from the quarters came, and owners of the tanyard. Old man Roland from his hut up the creek came with his seven hound dogs, long and lean fellows just like him in looks. It was always told he slept with his dogs and his chickens roosted on rafters over his bed and two sheep bedded down in front of the fire. We all cried for Mr. Paul. There was never a word about who he was. He had come alone, and he died without telling where he came from, but he had made a place for himself in our hearts. No more would we be looking for a relative of his to come to our farm searching for him."

Nighty-eight years is a long time to live, and Mary Martha Twilberry seemed to love all she could remember of it. Her life reminded me of lines I copied years ago from a book of poems.

> Age comes so gently to the folk
> who take it
> With peacefulness and understanding
> smiles,
> Age brings a blessing to the
> folks who make it
> A haven after long and weary miles.

The Hanging
of Bright Gibson

Ollie Spann told the following story:

"I well mind the day Samuel Grayson came riding into the south forty to tell me the news: Bright Gibson had been found guilty of murder and was to be hung three months from last Friday.

"When I saw Samuel coming astride his old sorrel mare, I thought how much he looked like a scarecrow, with his long black drooping coat and sagging moustache—even the brim of his old felt hat looked tired and ready to give up, worn way down almost to his eyes, which always seemed to be looking sideways. He was double cross-eyed, so said my mama, who was a cousin to his grandmother. Both his parents were cross-eyed and had a whole house full of children who were cross-eyed, and every last one still lived at home.

"Samuel was the sort of fellow that got no pleasure out of anything. Now he wasn't going to get one drop out of the most exciting thing ever to happen in our county. Samuel wouldn't bet on how many beans was in a glass jar, not even to help out at the school socials, so 'fraid was he that he would lose.

"And now he was going to lose the pleasure of killing Bright Gibson. The law was going to kill him. I minded how Samuel had talked about killing Bright for thirty years until folks round-about was tired of hearing the wrong Samuel thought Bright had done him when they were yearling boys. Thing is nobody ever found out what Bright had done to Samuel, other than 'he talked to me like I was a dog.'

"I was right put out it was old Samuel coming to tell me the hanging news, since he never discussed anything after telling the bald facts. I like folks who are like a dog with a bone—take it over there and bring it back, gnaw on it a bit and then take it off to bury it for a while, change their mind and dig up the bone to gnaw on, getting that good taste in their mouth. Now I am like that dog with the bone; I like to hash over news, get all the good out of it. Law, how I wished it had been Gabe Turner. Now there is a man who can think of more ways to tell a-body something!

"Why, I bring to mind one time at our house, my wife had baked a jelly cake, and Gabe praised that cake so many ways he ate almost the whole thing while my wife stood by cutting large slices everytime he said it was light as a feather, sweet as honey, and as pretty as the cook. I almost got up and slapped Cora for being so took in by Gabe. Now that Gabe is a news toter. When he comes by my house, I just hitch the mule in the shade and get ready for a good hashing over the settlement news.

"Right from the second I knew they was going to hang Bright, I wanted to talk about it, for something in my chest started a kind of flutter and bobbing around and never stopped until the day after the hanging and funeral.

"Now, mind you, I didn't have a thing against Bright; he was a simple kind of fellow, with light hair sticking up in little tufts all over his head with tufts over each eye in place of eyebrows. He had one glass eye and the other was skim milk blue. He should have been a little weakling of a fellow to match his mind. But nature plays some funny things on humans; she gave Bright a body as big as an ox, though his voice was like a little girl's, you know, kind of soft and scared sounding. Why, Bright could take a horse shoe and bend the points together, easy as I can tie my boot strings.

"It 'twarnt no trouble for him to snap Millie Suffer's neck with one hand. That was why they were going to hang him. 'Course there was plenty of fellows who would have liked to slap Millie or give her a shove when she sidled up to them even when their wives were watching. She would sweet-talk with arm pattings, give deep sighs and even invitations to come by and visit with 'Mama and me.'

"She was a good-looking woman, with real rosy cheeks and bright hair hanging halfway down her back, but she picked the wrong man when she cut her eyes toward Bright. He broke her neck, then throwed her body in a weed patch behind her mama's house.

"As I said, I never had nothing against Bright, but I had never seen a hanging, and I wanted in the worse way to go to the county seat and see this one. You might say I was under a spell in a way, since that is all I could think about. For a time I talked about this event day and night, until I caught my wife looking at me kind of funny. Right off I shut up, for I minded she had told her sister she thought I was losing my mind, and I didn't want to land at Whitfield, least not before the hanging.

"When I went to bed, I would lie there and imagine how it was in jail, bars all around and safe, but not for long. Why, Bright didn't have a worry in the world, didn't have to go outside when nature called, had his grub slid under the barred door, never had to listen to children crying because of being sick.

"Day times I had it different. I once went to the barn and knotted a plow line, put it around my neck with the knot behind my right ear, then sat on the corn sheller half a day while the children hunted and called for me. I mind how I went up in the barn loft, moved some hay and made marks on the wall with a stub of pencil the children had left in the crib when they was shelling a milling of corn. I made a mark for each day Bright had left before they were going to hang him. Each time I made a mark I would get out my pocket knife and sharpen the point so it would be ready to mark off another day Bright had to live.

"My vittles began to set uneasy on my stomach and somehow I couldn't relish the common food like I once had. You see, I am a big fellow and it takes a lot to fill me up. Even the children noticed how I would leave the chicken gizzards, livers and necks on the platter and kind of nibble on backs—just couldn't down a thing to strengthen myself. Strong coffee and buttermilk kept me going. Even my chewing tobacco turned against me.

"Now, things wasn't bothering Bright a bit; he sat in his cell and joked with folks who came to see him. They came every day. Once a man from below the Louisiana line rented a two-wheel buggy and drove to the county seat to stare at Bright.

"I went to town every day when I could slip away from Cora. Now, she has made me a good wife, but she couldn't understand a thing like I was going through, and to tell it true I didn't have words to tell it to her. You see, we came along before the time of doctors exploring a man's mind and explaining all these funny things that happen to a fellow. Seems like I have heard that queer things can happen to people when they are youngsters, lay festering in their minds for years and then suddenly come to the surface. If something like this happened to me when I was small, it sure did mark me.

"I mind as how I had never wanted to help with the killing and picking feathers off chickens for our dinners. After I heard about Bright, I started going to the coop and taking fryers out and then standing with the chicken's neck in my hand wanting to hurry and feel the sudden parting of the bones under the firm grip of my hand, yet somehow wanting to put off the delicious feeling of power it gave me.

"We had chicken every other day. When I helped to wring their necks I would think, This is the way it will be when Bright is hung.

I would stand there after the little girls had taken the chickens to dress. I would rub my hand down my overall leg and think, Can this be Ollie Spann wanting the days to hurry past so I can see a man die?

"The idea of the hanging was working in my brain all the time, just like the sharp teeth of a caged squirrel, always gnawing on the support bars of his cage. Day and night I could feel the hurt of the teeth of thought as they gnawed around the edge of my brain. I knew if the hanging day didn't arrive soon and the teeth got to the soft part of my brain I was a goner, so you see why I marked off the days in secret.

"I had seen my daddy die, saw him dragged to death by a crazy running mule, saw him hanging head down, his face bouncing and hitting on rocks and clods in the field to the creek ford and on to the pole barn. 'Course I was a little fellow, couldn't reach the handles of the plow good; no matter I was taking the place of a grown man the day my daddy whipped me and said, 'I ought to break your neck for running around that cotton and plowing half of it up.' Then he jumped on the mule, giving it a heavy kick in the flank, and the mule, half crazed with worrying with me, started running, and Daddy got tangled in the harness. It didn't break his neck, but folks said it was a wonder it hadn't. From then on I wondered how it would be to see a person get his neck broken.

"Time passed and I forgot about the whipping my daddy gave me and the desire of Daddy to break my neck. I grew up, married, and raised children. Then Bright Gibson killed that poor girl, and the court promised to hang him. I just had to see it.

"I remember I went to the jail to see the trap. When I was led up those iron steps, they whanged and sort of rumbled. Once we reached where the trap doors were, I darted out of the sightseers' line and stepped on the doors with steady confidence that they wouldn't drop on me. I looked around to see the hanging rope. I guess they didn't keep it out in the open for folks to see.

"The nights were the worst time of all; I had to lie there and pretend I was resting. I longed for Cora to press my hand and say 'I understand your trouble.' 'Course she couldn't know what a strange thing I was going through. If she had known even a little bit of it she would have sent our oldest boy across the field to her papa's house to come get her and the children.

"The day of the hanging came bright and clear. I walked every step of the way to town, got there before good daylight, had a place right outside the jail door so I could see good. They even let me go up to see Bright. He wasn't worried one bit, just chewed tobacco and spit. I mind how he missed the bucket more than half the time, and I wondered who was going to clean up after him. There was a good crowd there pressing around the jail—men, a few yearling boys, and lots of dogs.

"Bright's daddy stood off to the side under a cedar tree. He had his hat off and held it over his heart with a trembling hand. They said Bright's mama was sitting in a wagon just outside of town waiting for the hanging to be over so she and his daddy could take their son's body home to be buried in the old Gibson graveyard.

"The trap was sprung, and Bright dropped like a stone. There was a sharp dull snap, and the deed was done. Cold sweat broke out all over me. Everything turned black and I felt like I was going to have a spell of blind staggers. By the time I walked home I was feeling pretty fair, and within a month I was the same as always.

"Can anybody reading this tell me what was the matter with me?" 🔲

The Settling
of Shady Rest

In the year 1778, Elder L. Waggoner and his bride, Emmatrude, left Vincennes after the English had retaken it from Roger Clark.

Leaving the settlement (which was the first town to be established in what was to be the state of Indiana in 1816), Elder Waggoner and his bride floated down the Wabash River on a flatboat to a point in Kentucky where a horse was bargained for. The two rode through the wilderness for days and days, even weeks, without seeing a soul, except a few Indians slipping through the forests.

Little is known of the Waggoner couple for the next four years. A journal tells of how they tried to convert Indians to their religion, which seems to have been one akin to the Baptist.

We know the Waggoner couple made it to the creek that now bears their name, Waggoner Creek, here in Amite County. The journal tells of the cave-home they dug on a pretty hillside across a valley from the creek. More entries tell of a daughter being born—a bonnie lass if one could overlook the angry red mark just below the left ear.

Other writings tell of a month the wife (now the mother of three children) spent alone while Elder Waggoner walked to Natchez to buy things to keep body and soul together: gunpowder, shot, salt, flour and medicines he could not gather in the woods that would someday be called Shady Rest. On this trip he brought home an Indian who was blind in one eye and very lame. For three years the Indian stayed around the Waggoner cave, seeming pleased with parched corn coffee, sweetened with wild honey, given him when he stood outside the cave door and grunted.

A small bit of new ground was cleared each fall and winter with the help of Emmatrude and a new horse traded for in Natchez. Things began to pick up around Waggoner Creek. Always in the back of Elder Waggoner's mind was the thought of preaching to the Indians who lived in the woods around their little farm. A small lean-to, no larger than the ox stall, was built to hold service. No record was made as to converts to the Waggoner religion.

Came the time when Emmatrude must leave Waggoner Creek for a few months to be under a doctor's care. (She had been there for fifteen years and had never gone more than two miles from home.) The trip by ox cart took weeks over a trail through woods that at times seemed no more than an imagined thread of thought running into the deep and vast forests.

Emmatrude never came back to the small home of two rooms with daube chimney and packed dirt floors known as Shady Rest. A diary written in another feminine hand tells of how L. Waggoner's first wife did die of 'wasting away, with much blood spitting toward the last.' It also tells of how the writer married L. Waggoner the day he started homeward with the body of his wife, frozen stiff, for the winter months were indeed very cold. Imagine, if you can, a honeymoon trip with the body of the first wife and her children in a wagon pulled by two oxen, one very lame.

The keeper of the Waggoner home fires for well over fifty years bore Elder Waggoner some seventeen children. One daughter married into the Ervin family down Bayou Sara way, having many sons and three daughters. One of these daughters married into the Berryhill family; a daughter, Elizabeth, married into the Budd family, and that is where I came from.

In these days of modern travel when we zip great distances by car in cooled or heated comfort it makes one wonder how our foreparents dared to venture into the great unknown with only a horse, gun, wife and, if the journal is correct, a sack of salt, sack of corn, a change of dress for each, a piece of tanned leather to repair their shoes, an awl, five square nails and flax seed. Nothing is mentioned about the use of flax seed. One wonders why bring flax seed to the wilderness. 🖾

Waiting for the End of the World

In the same year that Mississippi was admitted to the Union, 1817, William Miller, who was an American seer, predicted that the world would end in 1843.

Preaching the doctrine of the second advent, he labored among all parties and sects without interfering with their organization or discipline and therefore touched many people.

At one time there was a letter in our family written to a forefather of mine from his grandfather who lived an eight-day journey from Vincennes, Indiana. I quote from a copy made of this letter:

"My dear kinsman, while I nor any of your kinsmen here in Indiana believe in the prediction of Baptist Miller that the world will end in 1843, one should give pause to the state of their soul.

"I trust you have seen to the salvation of the sons and daughters under your roof, and I pray your brother Samuel will see the light and turn to the Lord before it is too late.

"Did your Aunt Letticia write you about Benjamin and his family moving to New Harmony to join the new and perfect society being set up by Robert Dale Owen?

"Word came saying this society is based on a plan of each person contributing the same amount of work and sharing alike.

"It would be a sad state of affairs if all who join are as lazy as Benjamin and his sons. I predict New Harmony will be a failure.

"If William Miller is right in his predictions, we will never meet again, for your letter of two years ago told of plans to come for a visit in 1844."

My relative to whom the letter was written paid scant attention to the end of the world. He was having a hard time keeping his brood of twelve children fed and clothed. He and his friends, relatives, and neighbors had heard of Miller. Every year or so a wandering preacher would preach on the second coming of Christ, mentioning that William Miller, a seer, gave the date as 1843.

Came the great meteor shower seen over most of the United States, especially in the New England area, on November 11, 1843. Mass hysteria swept across the United States. Those nearest to the New England area left their crops unharvested, gave away their possessions and began leaving their homes, wandering on foot or in wagons, waiting for the end of the world.

In Summit lived several families who believed William Miller's prediction. When the meteor shower showed for several days in these parts they too began getting ready for the end. A man who lived in the Summit area owed my relative seventy cents. He made a two-day trip to Waggoner Creek to pay off his debt, bringing along two shoats and a young kid to give my relative, who held no truck with the "end of the world" predictions. It was said Grandfather tried to turn the man back toward Summit and failed. Hearing from the man that others in the area were giving away their worldly goods, Grandfather and his sons set out in wagons pulled by oxen hoping to bargain for things they badly needed and for a few wanted pretties.

The list sent along by his wife was around for many years: spinning wheel, candle molds, suet or beeswax, wool cards and wool fleeces, a water set, a pea hen and mate, milch cow with calf by side, a barrel of pickled pork, dried apples without worms, and a copper pickling kettle. The wagons came home with oxbows and yokes, scythes, demijohns filled with sorghum syrup, kegs of lard, bolts of red flannel, a feather bed, corn in the shuck, a wall mirror, and clothing for outdoor work.

When spring came and the world was rocking on, many of the givers came to beg for their things to be returned. Old-timers (my kin included) were always ready to turn a penny. They charged board for the fowl and animals and storage for the household plunder. The food had been eaten and the feather bed burned as it had chinch or bed bugs in it.

William Miller's predictions were handed down through the years. In 1933 believers living near Summit were preparing for the coming of the end of the world as did their foresires in 1843. I was a freshman at Southwest Jr. College at Summit. I was seventeen years of age and certainly not ready for the end of the world. A classmate brought a note to the late Mr. Kenna (president of the college) asking to be excused from class one day in November. She whispered to me that her family, including herself, believed the world was coming to an end the next week, and they had much praying and fasting to do.

Sure enough, the shower of stars came as it has done every hundred years since recorded events are known. However, the sun rose the next morning as usual. Strong of faith, this family spent the day in prayer and fasting. When dusk came, the oldest son was sent to the barn to throw down hay to the bawling cattle, which had been without food or water for two days. On his way back to the house, he was suddenly startled by a green light, followed by a ray of red. Then a clear white swath passed overhead. Believing the end of the world was truly upon him and his family, he began running and calling. The family came outside to look toward the east where the lights were coming from; strong and true came the flashes of light green, red, and white over and over.

My classmate told me that she was sure the next few minutes would be her last. She and the whole family were ready with no fear, so strong was their faith. She remembered that she had not memorized a poem for class and wondered if that would be held against her. Weariness overcame the family, and all went to sleep. The sun came up, and again the family prayed. The younger children were given food and drink while the older members prayed and fasted.

When early dusk came, the mother walked to the mailbox, about a half mile each way, to get the weekly newspaper. When night fell, the flashing lights began to show. The mother decided to cook supper, and waiting for the biscuits to bake, she began reading the front page of the paper. She read: "McComb, Mississippi, is on the map. Beacon lights for airplanes were turned on Wednesday. Each night the flashing red, green and white lights will be seen over the whole area. It is assumed many will be wondering what this strange flashing is—nothing more than progress for our community."

The whole family took the news with good grace. My classmate said she got busy learning the poem because Monday was the day she was supposed to recite it, and having Miss Earnestine Tommye give her a hard look was honestly more terrifying than thinking the end of the world was coming. 🖼

Dancing Girls and a Fire-Breathing Dragon

T he following story is one heard around low-burning fires when adventures are told. I do not vouch for the truth of the events, said to have happened to a relative of mine over 137 years ago.

It seems word had drifted to the Budd household that Commodore Matthew Perry would accept boys of high esteem for sailing to Japan, where he had the task of getting one or more ports open for American ships. Being as young Daniel had adventure in his heart and one year at the United States Naval Academy, he felt well qualified for a place aboard ship. He was accepted and sailed to Japan with Commodore Perry in the year 1853, arriving there on July 8.

It was told that the Japanese weren't too cordial, and that the ship sailed on to China to give the citizens of Japan time to study Perry's proposals. The ship and its crew returned to Japan in February, 1854. There is where Daniel got into the trouble that caused his mama to whale the daylights out of him the first few minutes after he got back home, even before he had time to unpack his trunk and pass pretties to eleven younger brothers and sisters gathered around the huge fireplace.

When Daniel had left home five years before to go around the world with Perry, his family lived in Indiana, on the Wabash River, where farming and barrel staves were made. These staves were floated down the Wabash River, into the Ohio River, thence to the Mississippi River and down to New Orleans where the staves were made into barrels. These barrels were sold to whiskey and molasses people who used them in their businesses. The Budd men fell in love with the lands they saw along the way as they walked from New Orleans to Indiana and decided to move to Mississippi where relatives had settled much earlier.

Daniel was advised of the move via letter that took three years to reach him. However, after his parting with the navy he came to Waggoner Creek. He stepped into the big room lighted by jumping flames. After he kissed his ma and bowed to his pa, he removed his coat to let his family see how large he had grown—alas and again alas, one of his shirt sleeves rode up his arm, showing vivid tattoo marks.

He was ordered to take off his shirt, and to his mother's eyes when he rippled his muscles, the fire-breathing dragon and a dancing girl seemed to be alive. She and his father had forbidden him to get a tattoo. Now he had two. It mattered not that she was a tiny woman and Daniel a strapping fellow of six feet. Quicker than you could wink an eye, she turned him over her knee and gave him a good paddling.

Turning to the seven sons who stood with bugged-out eyes, she said, "Let that be a lesson to you—don't ever get yourself tattooed. If you do, I'll wallop the stuffing out of you." Five of the seven sons went to sea and not one got a tattoo.

It is told that Daniel entertained his children and grandchildren with the fire-breathing dragon and the girl from Japan dancing up and down his arm. Daniel had had himself decorated with one of the oldest personal adornments known to man: some Egyptian mummies from 1300 B.C. bear blue tattoo marks under their skin. ▓

The Turkeys in the Red Flannel Suits

The story goes this way: Grandmother Budd made sure her pantry was well stocked with fruits, berries and vegetables from the farm. Several gallon jars of blackberries were put up fresh to use during winter months for pies, cobblers, and cakes, and if the jelly or jam shelf got low, these same berries could be used for making suitable sweets.

When one jar was opened, it proved to have fermented, as did the second, third and fourth gallons right on down to the fifth and sixth. The berries were emptied into a large tub and sent to the pasture. Instructions were given to bury the berries in a deep hole, so that no animal might eat them and get sick. Whoever was supposed to bury the berries simply poured them into a ditch, then moseyed to the house with never a word to Grandmother that her instructions had not been followed.

Sometime during the afternoon hours, Grandmother's prize flock of turkey hens and fine gobblers went sashaying off to the pasture to preen and strut about. They found the berries in the ditch and ate their fill, perhaps more, for the taste was delicious to the birds. They managed to stagger to the barn before passing out in a deep stupor.

Not knowing what caused the apparent death of her beautiful fowl, Grandmother, always one to take an opportunity to get feathers for her feather beds and pillows, had them dry picked. She instructed those picking the hapless birds to toss the naked fellows in the ditch where they had eaten the food that made them the way they were, drunk as the proverbial Cooter Brown.

Early afternoon saw the turkeys homeward bound for corn and roosting in the huge pecan trees in the back yard. Imagine Grandmother's dismay when she saw naked turkeys walking about! And on the way was another big freeze (so said the almanac)—one that would freeze the horns off a billy goat, which meant a real ground spewer.

Every female on the place who could thread a needle was put to work cutting flannel suits to fit the plucked birds. (Seems as if several bolts of flannel were kept on hand for winter underwear.) One of my great-aunts remembered that night as one of the most

fun-filled times of her life: big fires burned in the kitchen and dining room fireplaces, the Home Comfort iron range was kept going
all night, the tall granite coffee pot boiling, sweet potatoes roasting
in fireplace ashes, and peanuts parching in the stove oven. Popcorn
popped and Grandmother agreed to a small platter of syrup candy
to pull.

Finally all of the fowl boasted red suits sewed on with stout thread.
My aunt told us of how cold it was outside, how white the moonlight,
almost as bright as day. As each turkey was suited, it would be taken
outside and put on a low limb of the tree where it could go higher
and sleep for the rest of the night.

Aunte Sukie (bless her heart) made a bit of hairpin lace to make
a frill around Ole Buster's neck opening; she also put a sassy little
pocket on the left side of his suit. Grandmother said the lace didn't
last out the daylight hours the next day, for the other turkeys ganged
up on Buster and picked off the lace a bit at a peck.

The red suits lasted until enough feathers were grown back and
warm days were just around the corner. 🎋

The Truth about
Pete's False Teeth

M ary Rollins, barely a kissing cousin, wailed that her granddaughter, age six, was going to be the world's youngest wearer
of false teeth. Visits to the dentist six or seven times each year
resulted in two or three cavities filled each time. Mary said she began
wearing false teeth at thirty-two, and that her daughter, soon to
be thirty-six, was on the verge of being fitted for "store-bought"
teeth. Seemed as if bad teeth ran in the Hillare family.

She showed me a picture of great-great-grandmother Pete, showing
a mouth full of gleaming teeth. The picture was taken when Pete
was twenty, so said the faded writing on the back. Mary continued
musing about her foreparent who lived to be 100 and was able to
thread a needle two weeks before her death (she was sewing a ruffle around the neck of her to-be-buried-in dress). Another picture
showed Grandma Pete at age ninety-nine with a pronounced smile

showing a lot of flashing teeth that looked the same as they did seventy-nine years before. Mary continued with the story of the woman who was a distant cousin to our family.

Born to parents long past their youth, Pete grew, waxing healthy and strong. Born with two lower teeth, she was considered something special. No matter the agony she caused her mother at nursing time—the teeth were left in because her doting father loved to brag about them. He also told how Pete began walking about the dirt-floored cabin at nine months, speaking words at one year, and singing herself to sleep with little made-up tunes at fifteen months.

It was certainly nothing to brag about that she had no teeth at age five, not even the two milk teeth she was born with. Various home remedies were brewed, all in the interest of causing teeth to "come through." Old books were searched for magic cures, and strangers were asked for advice in case they had heard of such a dilemma.

Pete's father made a month-long walking trip to below Bayou Sara to learn firsthand from a man said to have cut his third set of teeth. If the food, water, herbs or even the weather had wrought this miracle, Pete would board with a distant relative living in the same area, thereby growing herself teeth. Alas, the trip was for naught. Four new teeth had appeared in the man's mouth—wisdom teeth cut at age seventy-five, long after he had been toothless for years.

These were hard times for farm folk who had no money and nowhere to go for help even if there had been cash stashed away in the side of the dirt-mud-daubed chimney. Very little food for a toothless child was to be had; her parents were also on the verge of being hungry all the time. It was a chore to get enough food to stay alive.

The year Pete turned nineteen she became very ill with high fever and a rash covering her body. Her mouth was inflamed with swollen gums and was covered with firm lumps that almost drove her crazy.

Tales told around low-burning fires of my childhood referred to a paper kept by the old mother that went this way: "Pete is burning with fever—she begs for something to gnaw on hoping to ease the pain of her gums. A ham bone gives her much comfort."

A doctor had opened up a small office to tend to the sick and ailing. Pete's father walked to the settlement and asked the doctor to come with him to lance his daughter's gums. Weeks later teeth were coming through the lanced places. In the following year, Pete grew a complete set of beautiful extra-white teeth so perfect that those who met her for the first time would say, "Such a pity, false teeth and so young." Pete cleaned her teeth and massaged her gums with a frazzled black gum stick and chewed sweet gum when she passed a tree with oozing gum.

After Cousin Pete died, the story was told in our family for many years of how the doctor, who came to see her an hour or so before her passing, was greeted with a weak but white-toothed smile.

He said, "Why don't you let me have your teeth? I believe you will be more comfortable without them."

Always one for a little joke, Cousin Pete opened her mouth for the doctor to remove her teeth. The doctor tugged and tugged, then asked what she used to hold her teeth in. She replied that God helped her keep her teeth.

A family member said the doctor leaned closer to peer into Cousin Pete's mouth to see for himself that her teeth were real. When she told him she had never had a cavity and there were four wisdom teeth to be cut if she should live so long, the doctor muttered, "I have heard of real-looking false teeth, but this is the first time I have seen false-looking real teeth!"

Kissing cousin Mary should hope her grandchildren inherit teeth like their great-great-great-grandmother Pete. 🏵

Child's Play

Trapping Schemes

Yesterday my mind went winging to the past almost sixty-five years ago to a time when my father oiled up his traps and took to the fields and streams, hoping to add a bit of money to the family income, which at that time was nothing. The harvest that fall was lean, not nearly enough to pay off the bank—much less to buy the enameled rug Mama yearned for, or the patient doctor who had come miles to look at our tongues and measure out pink and white powders, not once but several times.

There was scarcely enough to keep the wolf from the door in things necessary to a semblance of half-way living. Mama was even more careful than usual of salt, coffee, spices and tea; sugar was bought in 100-pound bailing sacks that would weep and drip when the weather was damp. The man who was supposed to collect for a fine pair of mules bought on credit came in November, taking away gallons of syrup, two wagonloads of ear corn, a coop of hens and a tough old rooster, three sheep, and four hogs as part payment, along with a promise to do better when the next harvest came.

Needless to say, the bulk of animals caught in Daddy's traps were rabbits. The tenant folks and the Budd family got mighty tired of rabbit—we had it in hash, stewed, fried, and pickled. Mama, desperate for eggs to sell to buy our school supplies, began using rabbit in place of hens to make chicken pies and salad. Using boiled dressing, boiled guinea eggs, and homemade pickles, a tasty sandwich would be made for school lunches. Rabbit pie was made the same as layered chicken pie: delicious with butter, broth, salt, lots of pepper, and sometimes tiny white onions.

Daddy kept hoping for a mink hide, which was said to bring at least two dollars. The one he caught was sickly, the hide riddled by wolves and covered with fleas. He didn't bother to dress out and stretch the hide. A letter went off to the state house for a permit to set beaver traps in Waggoner Creek; it had been told a beaver hide would bring ten dollars. We never found out, for the beavers were too sharp to be caught in the huge cage-trap affair.

There were exciting tales of easy money for small hides, namely squirrels. Brother and I whittled boards to stretch hides from the many squirrels brought to the backyard to be dressed for table food. From somewhere, we learned, forty hides later, that there was nothing to this rumor. However, a man was on his way to buy squirrel tails. This fellow was known as a "swapper and trader," dealing not in cash but in toys and sweet goodies to swap for good-quality tails.

We wailed over the many tails we had thrown away and at once began saving them, pressing them between two worn-out whetstones, the kind with a big hole in the middle. When the tails were dry we would tenderly place them in an empty shell box. Every night we would drag out the box, take the tails out and count them over and over, making a stack on one side for Brother and a pile on the other side for me.

We looked for the swapping and trading man every day, adding more tails as we wandered far afield asking neighbors for the tails from their hunting trips. When we left for school we would caution Mama to drive a hard bargain for us. We planned to sell the candy and toys to neighbors and buy a bicycle with the money. We never once thought where the poverty-stricken neighbors would get even a few copper cents.

The swapper man never came. After a year or so, the box of tails was carried to the smokehouse and put on a top shelf.

Once in a cleaning bout, Mama had Marianna, her daily helper, throw the moth-riddled tails in a deep ditch. The shell box with the original red printing on the sides is now a conversation piece. Shell boxes aren't made out of good pine lumber nowadays. 🈴

Coupon Treasures

In my pre-salad days Mama was a saver of soap coupons. She outfitted her kitchen with dishes, pots and pans, graters, company table spoons, a best tablecloth, even a pretty lamp for the sideboard. All these free things were brought into the family with coupons saved from a famous yellow bar of laundry soap called Octagon and its companion washing powder, Golddust.

The children in our family had the pleasure of looking over the coupon book to select what we wanted for our birthdays or for gifts for relatives who lived in big towns and sent their laundry out to be done.

Counterpanes for 300 coupons were favorites with housewives; these beautiful covers with raised designs could be ordered by number or name. "Broken Fence," in snow white, was Mama's pick. We didn't dare jump on a puffed high feather bed when it was made up, complete with pillow shams and the counterpane, for Sunday company.

A ring for my eighth birthday cost fifty coupons. I recall Mama sending me across the creek to borrow five coupons from a neighbor to finish out the order. I wore the ring for years. My sisters Bess and Rhoda took their turns wearing it—in fact, it was passed along to them as a birthday present.

Dinner plates were ten coupons; silver-plated knives, forks and spoons cost only twenty-five coupons each. Beautiful pieces of majolica ware for jellies, pickles, candy, and relishes were sent for and given as Christmas presents. One of my favorite things is a piece of majolica ware in the shape of a cabbage leaf, green with heavy veins of lighter green, bordered by spicy lavender.

When Mama's heart desired something special, she felt she could not wait to collect coupons a few at a time, so she would take her saved butter and egg money and buy several cases of soap at one time. We had a wonderful time unwrapping the soap, then stacking it on a shelf in the smokehouse where it would dry out and would last much longer than usual, getting so hard it never melted away as did just-opened soap.

The soap wrappers were stored flat, the better to cut around the edges of the coupons. If we left too wide a piece of the wrapper we were told to trim again. Didn't we realize it would cost more to send unnecessary paper? We learned arithmetic—each bundle of coupons must not contain less or more than twenty-five. We added, multiplied and then divided to arrive at the total of 750 coupons.

We yearned over lockets in the shape of hearts, some with chip diamonds. Others had wee hinges and opened, showing places for pictures. No matter how much we begged for a wrist watch with black silk cord band, Mama never considered sending 1,000 coupons for this unnecessary article. Neither did we get a folding comb in a silver case hanging from a decorative pin which was supposed to be pinned to the shoulder. How I longed for a fountain pen with cord for wearing around one's neck. For boys there were footballs, tennis rackets, tweed knickers, and leather belts with gold buckles (for thirty-five extra coupons one could get up to three initials on the buckle).

Mama longed for a rug to go in front of the fireplace (summertime only, when there were no fires)—a rug made of soft yarns, picturing a white fluffy kitten tangled in a ball of blue yarn. It was only 375 coupons. One Christmas Santa brought Mama this rug and left it under the Christmas tree. For several years I was happy to know Mrs. Santa used Octagon soap and Golddust for her washing at the North Pole. 🎴

Searching for
Dirt Dauber Houses

A t the back side of the mule lot on our place when I was small was a peeled-pine-log crib, used at one time to store corn when bins overflowed at the big barn at the end of harvest season. The little crib was used by Mama to store dried feathers for making pillows and refreshing feather beds when they became limp and doughty. In the fall, broom straw was stored across the rafters after it had been cured in the fall sunshine.

High off the ground was the crib, and each wooden block had a flared cap of tin made in an effort to thwart rats who gnawed and ruined; in addition, the cracks between the logs had been daubed with a mixture of red clay, lye, tar, and moss.

Evidently these measures didn't work, for Mama was careful to hang from the rafters anything she didn't want rats to gnaw. Using pieces of bailing wire to suspend them, she stored items such as wooden lard paddles (used only in winter when hogs were killed and lard was stewed down) and the heavy wood floor-scrub board, which had holes made in orderly rows to be stuffed with shucks. When scrubbing day came, a green gum handle would be whittled and placed in the slanted handle hole. This board, along with white creek sand, lye soap and plenty of elbow effort, kept the long porches and kitchen floor clean and white.

The scrub board interested Brother and me one hot summer day when we were sent to fetch it from the crib. Every hole had been sealed with mud, so smoothly and cleverly that it was hard to tell where the holes were. Uncle Jack came to our rescue by taking his knife and reaming out the holes, giving us a nature lesson on the way dirt daubers saw to it that their babies would have plenty to eat until the time came for them to emerge into the world: out tumbled live spiders, green pieces of leaves, and the unhatched daubers.

Uncle Jack believed in keeping children busy, quiet, out of the way, and out of mischief. When we became fretful he would let us bore holes in the pine poles of the crib using an old brace and bit, an auger, and a gimlet, all the while telling how the flitter wasp, dirt daubers, and other wasp kin would be happy to find these holes ready for their egg laying and baby raising.

Uncle Jack offered a prize to Brother and me for the most unusual types of dauber nests (the mud kind) we could find. We would creep around the sides of houses, barns and any likely-looking places where such nests would be built. We spent a whole summer collecting nests and protecting them in shoe boxes given to us by our Uncle Welch, who ran a store in Liberty.

Some daubers made messy nests, pasting little daubs of mud to make a polka-dotted affair that wouldn't stand a good shower of rain. Others made long tunnels of mud with sideway ridges, and there were pudding-shaped nests divided evenly into sections almost as nicely as an orange. Some nests were tri-part and some had five tunnels. Evidently many daubers were in a hurry and made nests by stopping up key holes in doors to rooms not used often.

One very lazy dauber had utilized an abandoned wasp nest, smoothing mud over it until it resembled a huge dirt flower. I thought that find would win me first prize. Brother spied an old felt hat left hanging in the harness room at the big barn. This hat was trimmed with pudding-shaped nests completely around the sagging brim, and the oval crown was encased with tunnels curved to fit the crown. Of course the dauber hat won the prize—a fishing trip to the upper place branch where mud cats were fat and anxious to bite our baits.

Aunt Mariah was very proud of "store-bought, ordered-off" teeth, reserving them for once-a-month church going. They were stored over the top shelf at the back porch waterhouse. Imagine her surprise to discover that a dauber had made a nest inside her teeth, between the upper and lower plates, sealing the plates together in such a clever way that she didn't have the heart to break up that old dauber's housekeeping. She went to church toothless. 🎏

Aunt Eula and a Wonderful Childhood Easter

O ur aunt Eula had no children, but she and her husband Leslie made sure there would be Easter eggs for the annual hunt given for their nephews and nieces.

Aunt Eula had a blue purse, called her "egg purse"; this small money holder fitted into her large bag, which she "toted" over her left arm. When we were given a nickle or penny, this money always came from her egg purse. "Goodie food," as we called it, was bought with egg money: a hoop of cheese, a case of macaroni, a large tin box of salty crackers, a large can of oil sausage, and a case of pink soda pop. These were used to make a quick and easy meal when company came just before sitting-down time. The soda pop was for children only, as her coffee was too black and strong. Grown men had been seen to stagger after drinking two cups of her home-parched and ground coffee.

Every year we were invited to the Toler home on Friday before Easter for an afternoon egg hunt. Their lawn was velvet smooth, and around the edges were side beds filled with larkspur, snapdragon, tiger lilies, thrift, and other country-loving flowers—perfect places for tucking colored eggs out of sight. We looked forward to this outing and were on our best behavior. Mama curled our hair and we wore our last year's Easter clothes.

On this fateful Easter it was discovered that I had grown fat during the winter so that my old Easter dress wouldn't button down the back. How it hiked up in front! The sleeves bound my upper arms until I felt faint. There was nothing to wear except my new Easter frock. Brother and my sister Bess set up a howl to wear their new clothes. With Mama almost in tears and her children smiling and happy, we set off in Grandmother Budd's buggy, pulled by fast-stepping Big Annie.

When we passed old Mrs. Mather's house, Mama prayed she wouldn't see us and rush out to talk. There was no way to get away from her—she simply took hold of the horse by the bridle and held on for dear life. Many is the time she walked along beside the buggy talking every step of the way. I never understood why she didn't let Mama tell her the news of the community if she was so lonesome.

We arrived at Aunt Eula's right after dinner to be met with bad news. Company had come unexpectedly on Sunday afternoon. Her hens became scared and upset by the visiting children who ran them all over the place, even deep into the woods. The hens hadn't laid one egg since, and there were no eggs for a hunt.

But! She had done the best she could, and what an Easter we had!

Aunt Eula had baked dozens of cookies in various shapes: rabbit, hen, duck, and ovals like eggs. Tinted icing graced every cookie, and coconut was sprinkled on a few of the little chicks. There was also cocoa fudge and peanut candy. The table decorations were dreamy. Fresh flowers stood in the center of the table, and crepe paper streamers coming down from the coal oil lamp hung over the table to the backs of our chairs. We had place cards with our names—even our baby sister in the high chair had one, though it would be at least four years until she started to school.

At each plate was a small glass hen filled with wee hot biscuits, split open with a tiny piece of ham tucked in. Cheese straws, candy, the decorated cookies, and bottles of soda pop completed our refreshments. In place of eggs hidden in the flowers, Aunt Eula had made up a package of money for each child: three nickles and a silver dime—untold wealth to us! This would be money to spend when we went on our fall jaunt to Liberty in October to buy our school books and winter shoes.

When we were leaving, I told Aunt Eula, "I don't care if your hens never lay again." Her reply was, "If they don't lay, there will be no Easter party next year. I did all this with my egg money."

Looking after
Cousin Candy

C ousin Candy lived in a blue-shuttered house with four small rooms, each as square as an old-time tin cracker box. She kept the house as clean as the proverbial pin, with peacock feathers in pretty vases on the mantle of the front room and fresh flowers in season on a twig table in the tiny hall. A welcome sign, carved with oak leaves and acorns, hung just outside the front door.

Mama and Daddy, along with our grandmother Budd and maiden aunt Phleta, "looked after" Cousin Candy. Each morning in the summer when we were out of school, Mama sent a jar of warm sweet milk down to this loved cousin. On Thursdays, we also took a bucket of fresh-churned buttermilk with a pat of butter floating sweetly in it. Most of the time we were allowed to spend a while visiting and doing things for Cousin Candy, as she was getting along in years, so said Mama.

First I fetched her teeth from the dresser where they grinned at us from a water-filled glass. Brother would scoot to the back porch to bring a broom to brush up the hearth. Then he would rake out a few live coals to warm up the coffee pot. Cousin Candy, by her own admission, "wasn't worth a thing until a few sips of coffee are in my innards."

We looked for her glasses which were always under the extra pillow on the bed. Her walking cane was hooked over a knob of the marble-topped bedside table. To me the best fetching of all was lifting her switch of human hair from the bureau and letting it ripple over my hands in shining waves of pure white. She had naturally curly hair that never grew longer than the bottom of her ears—hence the switch to make a big fat bun, held to her head with long bone pins.

Brother was sent to the smokehouse to let the rat terrier out. It danced along on its hind legs, having been born with no front legs. While Brother was gone, Cousin Candy dressed under the tent of her long, billowing night gown. Emerging, she tied on a coverall apron and washed her face and hands in a wash bowl that was part of a set decorated with beautiful yellow roses.

While she drank a cup of warmed-over coffee she began giving us directions for helping, such as: "Let the lop-horned cow out of the first stall, shuck ten ears of corn for the pen hog, sweep the back porch and steps, start a quick corncob fire in the little stove." (The "little stove" was so small the oven would hold only one biscuit tin on its tiny rack, and there were only two eyes to cook on. Her Home Comfort range was complete with warming oven, copper-lined water tank and six eyes; the two racks in the oven could hold three cake tins each.) These runnings and fetchings for Cousin Candy were part and parcel of our lives. We never grumbled about doing these things, for we were being taught to "help out and look after old folks."

If doing for Cousin Candy with her cheerful way and fat sugar cookies and being told by Grandmother Budd that we were "blessed children" wasn't enough pay, twice each year packages came for Cousin Candy with presents inside for Brother and me, as well as clothing, books and magazines for her. Now that I am grown and full of wonderment about many things, I would love to know what she wrote about me in the letters sent to kinsmen who lived, it was said, "across the waters," which I learned later only meant the Mississippi River.

Did she say I was a freckled-faced fat child with a heart of gold? Did she tell I was longing for a hand comb to keep my fine cornsilk hair in order and a band comb with blue sets to hold the combed hair out of my eyes? Did she tell I wanted a heart-shaped locket with a chip diamond in the center, a pink purse with a turtle snapping closing, and roll elastic garters? Did she mention how I waited on her hand and foot the year she had measles (caught from me) when she was ninety-one? Perhaps she did, for the above pretties came my way the years I was eight, nine, and ten.

I never questioned whether she was our cousin. She was the only person I knew who had no brothers, sisters or relatives other than those called "cousin" right here on and near Shady Rest.

However, I do remember Grandmother Budd saying to her oldest living son, Uncle Ben, "Don't speak so plain about Candy. Remember, little pitchers have big ears." For some reason I knew she was calling me a "little pitcher" when I was trying to be quiet as a mouse, out of sight, as I played under the kitchen table, which was covered by a floor-length cloth. 🎴

Unusual Pets

Once upon a time Brother and I found pets so unusual that we were the talk of the neighborhood. This discovery occurred when we were strolling along at the edge of the upper place. Sunlight was twinkling on every blade of grass. Our feet scuffed fallen rusty leaves, and our noses tingled from the faint smell of the good earth.

We came into the scrub a little higher than our waists. Suddenly we heard soft clickings and smothered gulping sounds coming from a fallen log we knew to be hollow, since we had played many a game of crawling through it. Tiptoeing close to peer inside, we saw three baby buzzards. They were snow white and beautiful to our pet-hungry eyes. The smell around the log was so awful it almost made us lose our dinner. We played with the babies for some time, until we heard the sound of the conch shell, letting us know it was time to drive up the milk cows. "Don't you fret, sweet babies, we will be back tomorrow," we said.

We came every day. Finally the buzzards began sprouting dark wing feathers, then tail feathers. When they began flopping out of the log, we solved the problem by piling brush and limbs at the ends of the log. Then we had to take over the feeding. Lucky little Budd children! An old rail fence was close by, and the zig-zag of the rails made delightful places for lizards and scorpions to take the sun. Brother and I spent much time running up and down the fence killing these creatures, which we fed to our buzzard pets. Finally we turned to fishing, keeping the branch banks lined with set hooks. How those birds did relish the small fish we caught.

We took our babies out of the log to let them walk and flop about. One day two of them took flapping, running starts and to their amazement began to fly to an old gnarled dead tree. They would come to us when we called, "Buzzie, Buzzie." Then we would shut them in for the night.

We became more bold with our pets and carried them perched on our shoulders to the dead animals that had been dragged to the animal graveyard. How lucky we were when Kyle Green's blind mule stumbled into an old dug well and broke his leg. Kyle was in a quandary over whether to swing the mule up and try to have the leg set or to have him shot. Blessings on the folks who talked against saving a broken-legged, blind, well-over-twenty-five-year-old mule. The well was so close to Kyle and Leathie's house the mule had to be dragged off. The mule was in good shape and made meals for our pets for a week or so.

One fine day we proudly carried them home, though we had misgivings in our hearts. Half-grown buzzards aren't the prettiest fowl in the world, but Mama and Daddy were rather good-natured about them. For two weeks our pets sat on the backyard fence and made flying sorties into the wide summer sky.

Once a cranky neighbor came calling, then left in a great huff when Pete, Repeat and Winchester sat on the fence and stared at her with hungry eyes for an hour or so. She was a victim of a shin sore which had been on her leg for many years; it did smell to high heaven.

Before the third week ended, our pets left for parts unknown and never came to Shady Rest again. ▨

Bitten by the Circus Bug

B ack in my pre-salad days—in fact, the summer before I was to reach the age of eleven in November—I dreamed of becoming a bareback rider in the circus. I could think of nothing other than riding around and around on a white horse—standing up, sitting down, jumping through circles of fire, or standing on my head on the back of such a horse. I dreamed of voices shouting my name and a steady clap of hands begging me to ride my horse once more, to thrill the crowds with my graceful stance as I guided the horse with pressure from my toes.

You see, my father had made good his promise to take Brother and me to the circus in Gloster, a promise given us in return for helping Mama the whole summer. She was expecting a baby the latter part of July and couldn't run and fetch as she usually did. We were to keep plenty of trashy stuff in the wood box to make her canning pressure cooker keep up steady puffs of steam, to remember to feed the chickens, to gather eggs several times a day, and to keep the garden sass picked in time for dinner cooking.

When the day came, we arrived in Gloster around seven in the morning, having left Shady Rest some three hours earlier. We had taken no lunch, for we expected to eat goodies offered at the circus grounds; however, since the circus hadn't arrived from Baton Rouge, we ate fried egg sandwiches from Pop Hill's cafe.

Brother and I had a seat on a low-hanging limb where we watched the setting up of the circus and thrilled to the bareback riders who polished their routine nearby.

The next day at home I began my training, getting ready for the following summer when I felt sure I could join the circus and be assured of a steady job. First off I begged Daddy to trade his beautiful grey saddle mare for a snow-white horse. While Daddy was in complete agreement and even helped me with rigging up a very low jump for practice, he drew a firm line at swapping horses.

Right at first I kept falling off or jumping down when I started to slide or wobble—of course I sprained my ankle and was laid up for a week. The next bout of riding saw me forgetting to duck when the horse went under a clothesline that had been raised up but not high enough—the line hit me at the collarbone and rolled skin off my neck, chin, and to the tip of my nose. I guess it would have scalped me, only I gracefully bounded off, making a bow and giving up bareback riding as a way of making a living.

The circus bug had bitten me, and I decided to become "the snake lady," who wore thin chiffon pants, full and gathered at ankles and waist, and rode around in a gold coach. Across the bosom of this lady was a jeweled garment sparkling with vari-colored stones. Her arms were left bare so the snakes that wrapped around and around her arms from wrist to shoulder could cling better, or so I imagined.

I decided to start with a pair of green lizards, the kind that "showed their money," turning from green to brown and back again according to their environments. These lizards were gently pressed on each side of their heads and then allowed to clamp their tiny jaws onto the lobes of my ears, one lizard to each ear.

Once I had mastered lizards, I went on to snakes. The chicken snakes and the black runners we were able to catch weren't having any part of my proposed act; they refused to curl, twine, or writhe around my arms or neck. The second we turned them loose they made a hasty retreat to the woodpile or went under the barn and cribs.

Several days later I gave up the idea of being a snake lady in the circus. We had gone with neighbors to a revival meeting in a near-by pasture, where the preacher showed his faith by reaching into a box and bringing out "a vile, mean, stinking cottonmouth, a rep-tile so lowdown even the devil gives him a wide path." The preacher had worked himself up to a foaming, ranting, singsong of a chant; when he lifted the snake aloft, he was promptly bitten on the nose.

The meeting broke up as others who had planned to show their faith by lifting the selfsame snake broke and ran across the pasture. I didn't have enough faith in my future to pick up the sluggish snake as it crawled across the pinestraw-covered ground. In fact, I put on so much speed I passed the preacher, as we fled from the area as if the very devil was after us. 🖾

Schoolyard Games

Hopscotch and jump-the-vine were two games that came into play when we started to school in mid-October. How well I remember being eight or nine when hopscotch became too easy to win.

Cousin Eunice Hinton would send two of the big boys to the woods behind the school to cut several long grapevines for us to jump. These vines, fully fifteen feet and longer, usually lasted until jumping fever was over.

We jumped to "hot pepper," "building a house," "high water, low water," "follow the squirrel," "there goes my true love," "count to 150," and others we made up, often changing the name in mid-stride or -jump. Sweat popped out on our faces, pigtails flopped, our breath came fast. We gritted our teeth to make 150 jumps with an extra to spare and a "high water" or two at the last.

Many times when one girl began to falter and almost stumble, others would yell to let Sallie or Mable take the tired one's place. Always the best jumpers were saved until last; if things got really tight, an extra girl would be put to jump until one missed and retired in disgrace. How we envied the last one jumping, who looked as if springs pushed her up and down. How lightly she landed on the balls of her feet, how her smiles flashed at the ones standing on the sidelines!

Many times the teacher held off knocking on the side of the schoolhouse to let us know it was time to come in with our books. If someone was jumping near 200, Cousin Eunice would be there to urge the jumper on.

When sides were chosen, the lucky one who got the top of the stick always chose Annie Dora Roberts—she was the best jumper at the school. I remember I was always the last to be called—I was a poor jumper. When it came time to throw the vine, however, I was special. I could throw so fast, giving "hot pepper" with never a quiver of my wrist. Often the person on the other end of the vine would cry "calf rope" and give up her place as a thrower. I loved "high water"—the jumpers had to pick up their legs!

We made pinestraw playhouses on the west side of the schoolhouse, where tall pine trees shed needles for our beds, dressers, chairs, stoves and tables. Rooms were outlined with long piles of pinestraw or broken green pine tops.

The boys were never allowed to bother us. Woe to a boy who decided to take a fast run through our playhouses; he was kept in at noon recess and wasn't allowed to look out the windows to see what he was missing. His friends were flying around on flying jennies, playing baseball or walking about on tommy walkers. Boys shot marbles, though not for keeps—the teacher counted the marbles before they began playing and then again when they came in from recess. Perhaps they did play for keeps on the way home.

There was no lunch room. Each child brought a lunch in a paper bag or tin bucket or wrapped in a newspaper package that was fastened by crossed broomstraws stuck through holes in the paper. Several of the big girls had "bought" lunch boxes, with their names painted on the sides. How I longed for a box with folding handles and my own name, Rose Budd, painted in red letters on the top. When our aunt Doll came from New Orleans one Thanksgiving, she brought a late birthday present for me—the longed-for lunch box, pink trimmed in gilt, with my name beside a yellow rose bud.

Miss Lena Dixon, the most beautiful teacher we had, often treated her pupils to molasses squares. The recipe, simple and tasty, has been around for over sixty-five years.

Take ½ cup sugar, ½ cup butter, one egg, one cup
molasses, 2½ cups plain flour, 1 and ½ teaspoons soda,
½ teaspoon salt, one teaspoon ginger, ½ teaspoon cloves
and one cup hot water.

Cream butter and sugar, add beaten egg and molasses
and beat well. Add sifted-together dry ingredients, stir
well and add hot water, beat until smooth. Batter is soft,
makes a fine cake. Bake in greased shallow pan for thirty-
five minutes in 350° oven or until a toothpick comes
out clean. Makes fifteen generous portions. ▨

Aunt Phleta's Peacock Ring

I vowed to do something about my fingernails before another visit
to Grandmother's house. My nails were red in strawberry season,
blue in blackberry and huckleberry time, and green when English
peas were in. I wanted my hands to look nice against the blazing
jeweled peacock ring our maiden aunt Phleta kept tucked away in
a red velvet ring box. I have no idea if the stones in the ring were
real; here in the present day it matters not. For many years, my
cousins and I cherished, loved and longed for (believed a queen once
owned) that beautiful ring. The ring was secreted under a pile of
go-to-meeting underwear in the middle drawer of a dresser in the
company bedroom, better known as the Blue Room.

When nap time came at Grandmother's house, there was never
begging or slipping off to do something more interesting. I would
take the blue granite wash pan hanging on a nail under the
waterhouse and my own bathcloth, towel and bar of homemade soap
to the back steps and give myself what was then known as a "spit-
bath." 'Tis true I often left as much dirt on the towel and cloth
(and myself) as I had washed off in the water. This was no bother
when I missed spots on feet and legs; an old sheet would be spread
over the company counterpane on the guest room bed. I would have
an old washed-out nightshirt that had been my long-dead grandfather's pulled over my head, and then I would be boosted up on
the high feather bed.

Once settled for my nap, I would be handed the red velvet ring box with domed lid and mother-of-pearl button, which, when pressed, would open the box. Surely the hinges on the ring box must have been the best in the world, since it was snapped open thousands of times when the Budd grandchildren and their cousins were growing up.

Auntie lowered the window shades and closed the wooden door, not for a nap as expected but for enjoyment of the glowing brightness of the dazzling jeweled tail and crown of the silver peacock ring, a sight to behold once the pearl button was pressed. I turned the long sleeves of the nightshirt to elbow length, so I could get the stunning effect of silver against my stubby freckled hands when I slipped the ring first on my middle finger and spread my hand against my knee. Then, admiring, I moved the ring from finger to finger until I chose to leave it on the thumb of the left hand. (Once I had seen a picture of a turbaned sultan with a jeweled peacock ring on his thumb.)

How the stones glowed: rubies, diamond, sapphires, emeralds, and one topaz, my birthstone. Fifteen stones in all made up the sweeping tail, and a rich red ruby was in place for the eye. The crown upon the head of the proud peacock glowed with five colors: red, white, green, blue and yellow. Surely the ring was made by someone who loved good workmanship, for there were tiny pierced holes between each jeweled feather in the sweeping tail.

Alas, I never did anything about my fingernails, which matched the stones in the ring— red, blue, green, and sometimes yellow from fruits and vegetables I helped pick and prepare for cooking.

Several weeks ago I saw an ad in a pulp magazine offering for sale a ladies' peacock ring said to "dazzle friends and relatives." Set with real simulated stones, complete with plastic mother-of-pearl button, this ring would be sent in a simulated red velvet box. No cash or checks, only money orders would be accepted.

The ring I knew when I was a child must have been real. Sixty-seven years ago there were no such things as simulated velvet or plastic pearl—at least I don't like to think so! 🎎

Blue Hole
and Water Wings

B ack in my pre-salad days there were many swimming holes in
Waggoner Creek. However, none was so beautiful, delightful,
icy cold, and appealing as the blue hole below the bridge. The blue
hole was named because the water seemed to be a shade of blue-
green caused by willows leaning to see their streaming tresses in
the smooth flowing water.

Our grandmother Budd, our father, and others who oversaw our
swimming efforts did not see eye-to-eye with most country people
who taught their children to swim by the time-honored method of
simply picking up the child, throwing him or her into deep water,
and yelling, "Swim out or cry."

Indeed not. Long before we learned to dog paddle across the blue
hole, we were furnished with swimming aids made by those who
cared enough for us to pound lids down on gallon syrup cans and
search out twenty-five-pound Angel Food flour sacks—two cans and
two sacks per child.

A can to a sack and the open ends of the sacks tied together,
and away we went, paddling around with the knotted sacks well
under our armpits, the cans riding high on each side of our chest.

Each child would have a personal set of can water wings. Woe
to a person who snitched another's wings; that was a double no-no.

Once we went to the swimming hole to find several youths from
another community swimming in our special blue hole and using
our water wings. They refused to come out of the water and give
us our prized possessions.

We couldn't go after them because we couldn't swim. To add
insult to injury, they sassed Icy Picket, who was with us to see that
we didn't drown (she couldn't swim a lick). However, we could chunk
rocks and that is just what we did! Every rock didn't hit a bobbing
head, but enough rocks raised knots to cause the unwelcome visitors
to yell "uncle." Once in shallow water, they walked out of the water
wings, which drifted downstream and came to rest against a fallen
log.

That night a neighbor came to our house with his children to
protest the Budd children's actions. My father pointed out the dif-
ferences in size and age: Brother was nine and I six, while the

neighbor's children were twelve, fourteen and fifteen. Daddy told the caller that his children were on private property (this was well before the day when a stream was considered fair game for all, as long as those trespassing, so to speak, stayed in the stream). The boys were told to stay away from our swim hole and off Shady Rest. The girl was welcome at any time to come and swim with us.

On days when Icy didn't feel like getting in the water, Mama wouldn't let us use our water wings. Before we left for the creek, Mama would take smut from the fireplace and draw rings around our legs just above the ankles. We were to stay in the ford or shallows and go no deeper than the smut ring.

Icy would take a long, limber, cane fishing pole to the creek. If we ventured one inch over the smut ring she would slap the pole on the water to remind us to return to the approved depth. She wasn't above giving our legs a sharp rap with the pole to give pressure to her vocal warning.

Her warning was, "You chaps better behave. Don't you know you could drown in shallow water? Your mama said it don't take more than a tablespoon of water to drown a person."

Being Bad
around Aunt Phleta

Our maiden aunt Phleta had a way with children. She paid not the slightest attention to a child who picked at his food, tugged at his mother's skirts, or whined for favors not to be granted. Auntie would butter a bite of tender biscuit crumb and dip it in the sugar dish, and before you could say "Jack Robinson," the child would be smacking the crumb and waiting for more, which often was the regular food others at the table were eating.

A child who was shy, hiding or burrowing his head in his mother's lap, was picked up into a pair of ever-loving arms and taken to the "junk" room where wonders awaited. Who could resist sorting squares of brightly colored material into piles of red, yellow, green, purple and blue? The checkered squares went on top of the cowhide-covered trunk that had come down the Mississippi River on a flatboat in the late 1700s. The flowered squares were placed in a hand-made dough tray, and those that didn't seem to have a home at the time of sorting were placed in the lap of "Miss Boo," a doll who belonged to every child visiting Shady Rest.

A child could iron colored tissue paper with a small toy iron kept on the back of the wood stove. That stove was kept fired up all day every day, or so it seems to me now. Cooking of some kind was always going on. Coffee was parched for tenants or for neighbors who didn't want to spend the time parching green coffee beans, or who didn't have the patience of Grizel, Job and Griselda all rolled into one small woman like Grandmother Budd. Shelled corn was parched and mixed with red hot peppers for the laying hens. Hot water was always on hand in the copper-lined tank on the side of the stove.

Auntie kept plenty of doll clothes that needed pressing in a small tin box. In nice weather a naughty child might be found outside using the small rope-bound wash tub, a rub board, and tiny bars of lye soap, then hanging the clean wash on a low line using wee clothes pins. All such items were made by Uncle Jack, who used a knife and "know-how" whittling.

The older children were punished with methods of doubtful value, such as standing in a corner, placing one's nose in a ring drawn on the side of the smokehouse, doing without dessert, wiping dishes, picking up chips for starting fires, shelling corn for going to the grist mill, pulling up bitter weeds, and picking off potato bugs.

Auntie certainly didn't believe in switchings for small children. Often her methods seemed unfair to the other nieces and nephews, the ones who happened to be good at that very minute Auntie was correcting the bad child. Auntie would say, "Well, the cookie churn is about empty. I guess John or Sally will have to help me." She would get out her mixings and sweet cookie cutters, turn a stand box over, tie an apron around the naughty child's waist, wash his hands, then put him to work creaming sugar and butter by hand— a delightful task. Roads, castles, and whatever could be dreamed up were patted out in the big mixing crock.

Time was of no importance when Auntie was correcting a child; she talked in soft low tones and worked beside the bad child. They broke eggs into a deep dish to be whisked into foaming yellow froth, skimmed sour cream from a brown crock of clabbered milk, sifted flour, and measured lemon or vanilla extract with care. Next came mixing, when often the child got the dough above his wrists. Then came the best part of all: rolling dough on a clean fifty-pound flour sack, dipping the cutters into flour, and making stars, moons, trees, chickens, and even Santa in July and rabbits in October. Pans almost as wide as the oven were greased with long strokes (finger painting before kindergardens were started in our part of the woods). Then came the careful placing of the cookies.

The good-acting children would be shut out of the kitchen. Often they huddled on porch steps, smelling the delicious odors and knowing they would share in the spoils of being bad. They thought up ways of being bad so they too could "take turns" and have special treatment.

The way I remember it in the years around 1920, being sassy and not doing dreary chores did pay off when Auntie corrected us in her gentle way. 🌠

The Armadillo Shell Sewing Basket

L ast night as I sat watching and waiting (when I spy an armadillo I wake Dale, who goes forth to slay this dragon-in-miniature), I remembered a sewing basket I yearned for when I was around eight years old.

In those days, we often visited the Mose Robinson home below Liberty for fellowship and delicious food. A son, Morris Robinson, lived over Texas way where armadillos were found. Evidently they were giving trouble there, as I recall Mr. Morris saying that people went out on hunts to try to reduce the armadillo population. He also told of a contest put on to see if something could be done with the pesky things once they were captured or killed. One idea that was advanced was to use the shell for making a sewing basket.

One Easter he brought his mother one of these delightful baskets. I fell in love with it, so much so that I thought of asking the Robinson family if I could come live with them.

When the armadillo was dressed, its tail was put in its mouth; the feet were pressed closely to the sides and the ears were gently flared out. The shell was given coats of varnish to make it slick and bright. The hollow made when the insides were removed was lined with pink sateen. Pockets were placed around all sides and sewed directly to the lining. In the pockets were spools of various colored thread, a tape measure, scissors in two sizes, a darning egg, a thimble, and a package of chalk in three colors—pink, white and blue. The basket also had a needle threader, sharp needles in five sizes (all with golden eyes), a wee reading glass, and a small Bible—each item in its proper pocket.

Whenever we visited I made a beeline for the front room, where the armadillo sewing basket sat in "Sunday best" splendor on a table holding several family photo albums. A sheet would be spread on the floor, and I would spend happy hours sitting there, removing things from the sewing basket pockets. I would arrange the pretties in a circle and dream of the time I would have my very own armadillo shell sewing basket.

Nothing was ever used from the basket—not one strand of thread was unwound from a spool, no needle threaded from the pack, no hips were measured with the tape measure that unwound from a round silver case. The pair of stork scissors never cut a worked buttonhole, the Bible was never opened, the spy glass was never used, except by me in my playing.

The basket existed as an ornament for the parlor and a plaything for me. Years later when I visited the Robinson home, I looked for the basket and was saddened to discover that it was shabby and faded. However, I still remember the pleasure the armadillo sewing basket brought me. I can hardly bear to write the words "three score years plus eight," the length of time that has passed since I first saw the armadillo sewing basket. 🖼

Exciting Trips
to Liberty

D id you have a happy childhood? I know I did, living in the
country, going to town once each month to take farm produce to trade out at the general store owned by our aunt Ode and
her husband, Mr. Welch.

My aunt Phleta drove her fast-stepping mare, Annie, red as dark
satin and as shiny. The buggy was black with red trim and sported
fancy rubber tires. We would start out before it got hot, hoping
to be at Aunt Ode's where we could pull out and let the mail rider
pass. Annie was scared of cars. Aunt Phleta would let me drive the
buggy on one stretch of the road where the ruts were so deep there
was no danger of the wheels jumping out.

I would wear my best everyday dress and my only straw hat with
a hole cut in the top so a plait could be pulled through, thereby
keeping the hat from blowing off when we went fast on a hard clay-
packed stretch of road.

I was so excited I could not eat breakfast. My grandmother always
made me a scrambled egg biscuit to eat about the time we got to
the Amite River, where Annie would drink at the ford and rest for
a few minutes.

My egg biscuit was wrapped in a red-checked napkin that had
seen better days, so much so that many of the red checks were thread-
bare. Grandmother always told me that if it got lost it wouldn't
matter. To my knowledge it was still around when she died.

Before we left home, Auntie would carefully pack the eggs in round
cheese boxes, layering them with cottonseed. The butter prints were
nicely wrapped in oiled butter paper, and then in a clean white cloth
dipped in fresh well water, the better to keep it cool. The butter
box went under the buggy seat out of the sun.

After the mail rider had passed, we would start on our trip again.
Once there, Auntie hitched the mare to a cedar tree behind the
post office, which was beside the monument yard. We spoke to Miss
Syble Stratton, the postmistress, who kindly asked about our family, especially Grandmother Budd.

Then came the wonderful fun of going to the store, where town
ladies were waiting for Auntie. They had standing orders for eggs
and butter, once it was traded out with Uncle Welch. Auntie finished

filling her list for snuff, chewing tobacco, coal oil, clay pipes, rice, dress material, and spices. Often she would need a dishpan, water dipper, and sweet soap. Mendets were often bought, as farm women used these to patch holes in their cooking pots made from enamel or aluminum.

After I had looked over the fruit, cookies, and canned goods and opened the drink box, my uncle would fix me a little lunch: a slice of hoop cheese, a piece of oil sausage direct from a three-gallon can of sausage and oil, crackers from a square tin box with layer after layer of saltines, a cold drink, and my choice of assorted cookies. I loved every bite and was stuffed full since it was so soon after my egg biscuit.

After Auntie had inspected my hands and mouth, I was allowed to cross the street to the Liberty Mercantile, run by Cousin Kate Terrell. He would invite me to try on the ladies' hats, kept fresh in a four-sided glass case with shelves. Then he opened brightly colored umbrellas and gave them a twirl so the air could fan my face. Next we went over to the grocery side where I selected penny pieces of candy for Brother and my sisters.

I left with pasteboard boxes of several sizes to use in a playhouse I was building in an old crib at Shady Rest. I also had a ripe banana, which I saved to share with Mama.

No matter that Liberty was a wide place in the road, as big-town folks said. It was wonderful—lots of people, electric lights, and pretty things in the stores. It would welcome me on the next monthly trip to town. 🏵

Couzin Cat and Kitty's Magic House

"Couzin Cat" Wilkinson and his wife, Kitty, lived in a great rambling house built way back when labor was almost free. The materials came from the home place about six miles to the west. The ground pillars were huge sandrocks, tall as I was at seven years of age. Three of these were stacked on top of each other at every corner, so the house towered very high off the ground.

The plans of Couzin Cat were big. Everyone knew his plans for the house were too grand, for his money came from the soil and was made by the sweat of his and Cousin Kitty's brows. There were rooms on the ground floor that had never been finished. The upstairs rooms were floored and partly finished with rough ceiling; the third story was nothing more than a shell with chimneys piercing through its darkness. They soared high above the rived board roof and were ornamented with rods said to keep lightning from striking the house.

The kitchen and dining room were a little world apart, joined to the house by a walkway, and roofed and latticed in. There were pot plants and hanging baskets made from mule muzzles lined with moss. The kitchen was a fairyland to me. Strings of dried red peppers hung from the rafters, as did sacked hams and sides of bacon smoked and dried to Couzin Cat's taste. A Home Comfort range sat in one corner, boasting a hot water tank that got the water so hot a body could dip some and scald a cat if the need arose, so said Couzin Cat.

A pie safe with pierced tin doors held goodies we never had at our house, at least not in such large amounts: a whole hoop of cheese wrapped in a vinegar-soaked cloth, triple-decker teacakes put together with great blobs of chocolate icing, a stone crock of fried-down patty sausage, covered with pure white lard, biscuits as big as a tea saucer, just right for making syrup- and butter-biscuits (called boley-holey or finger biscuits). We were welcome to help ourselves any time the hunger bug bit us.

Every Easter the Wilkinson couple surprised Brother and me with something special. One year there was a set of acorn cups and saucers for me and several acorn pipes for Brother. Another year our treat was little baskets of softly colored eggs, decorated in what we call today modern form, even though Cousin Kitty used onion skins, blueing, flowers, and crepe paper to get her colors. The suprise was inside—as we peeled the eggs with careful fingers, we found messages written on the egg whites. Cousin Kitty said she made an "ink" using one ounce of alum to one-half pint of vinegar. Next she took a small pointed paintbrush and wrote and printed on the shell of the uncooked eggs. Allowed to dry thoroughly, the eggs were then gently boiled for fifteen minutes.

The best Easter of all was the year our cousins gave Brother and me box turtles with their shells painted in colors and our names engraved on the underside of each with a sharp pocket knife. These presents were found in the woods and decorated just for us!

When we arrived at our home, a little board pen was made under a pecan tree for the turtles' safekeeping. Visitors seemed to find our pets rare and different.

Needless to say, the turtles kept themselves shut in their shells most of the time, coming out to nibble on the food we put down for them when no one was around. One morning they were gone; even though we searched far and wide we never found them. Three years later Uncle Jack, taking a short cut through woods at the upper place, picked up my turtle as it was crawling along.

How did I know it was mine? The colors were dim and faded, but my name was right where Couzin Cat had carved and dated it: April 4, 1920, property of Rose Budd. ▨

Watermelons, Shivarees, and Party Lines

White Lightnin'
and Strange Afflictions

M any years ago the following events took place within a six-
month period. No reason was ever given for the afflictions
put on these people.

A family in a certain community came down with this condition:
first, the two oldest boys began beating their old mother, who wasn't
much of a cook to begin with, cursing her for not seasoning the
food. Then whippings and much ugly talk took place.

The family lived way back in the woods and had little or no company who saw the mother. Finally word leaked out after the two
sons (ages forty and thirty-five) went to a country store to buy a
few groceries. Being fond of cheese, they bought a pound to go along
with crackers, then went outside to sit in the sun and feast. Suddenly the two rushed into the store yelling and cussing the owner
for selling cheese with no taste. The owner cut a slice, ate it, and
remarked that there was nothing wrong with the cheese (this is what
the old men sitting around later told the lawman who had been called
after the brothers beat the store man, putting a "doggone good whup-
ping" on him). The lawman sampled the cheese and was afraid to
say it was tasty.

On the trip to the farm the brothers said that their mother had
lost her mind and didn't cook food fit for a mangy hound dog to
eat, and that their pa was ready to quit his stilling and go over in
another county and take up with a maiden lady looking for a man
to be a real daddy to her three boys who were running wild. When
they reached the farm, the lawman told the old daddy he better
behave himself and forget the foolishness of going over into another
county and taking up with the maiden lady, that those boys of hers
would flay the hide off his back and rub salt in the flays—they had
been known to do that very thing to a salesman who came by and
made sweet eyes at their mama.

To make peace with the lawman, the daddy of the fighting sons
invited him to go along to the still hidden in a hollow way back
in an old field. Both drank of the clear white liquid dripping from
a copper worm into a good-sized brass container. The lawman took

a quart jar of the white lightning home as a peace offering.

He also laid down the law to the boys and the father to lay off the old lady, who was a pitiful person when she wasn't suffering with a black eye, bald spots where hair had been jerked out, and red stripes around her frail legs where the boys had played rap-jack with her using long keen switches. They laughed and told the lawman, "Bet she jumped high enough to get over that rail fence when we whipped her."

It wasn't long until the lawman began complaining that his wife couldn't cook anything fit to eat, and he too laid a heavy hand on his wife to teach her to mend her ways.

Justice will often be meted out in time, if those needing it are still around. The whipping father and his loutish sons were sent to the county farm so that their uncle (their mother's brother) wouldn't shoot them down like mad dogs.

The old mother left these parts and went to another state to live. She was put on the pauper roll for four dollars a month, which seemed like a gift from heaven. Now she could have a whole can of snuff, not a spoonful in a twist of brown paper from the country store, which had cost her two eggs.

The sons and their father had to work as they never had in their lives—up before day and toiling in the fields until after dark. They began to complain about the food when they ate their first meal at the farm. They were ready to beat up the cook, a tall heavy-set man. Once he looked at them and then at the machete knife standing in a corner of the kitchen and said, "I used it once and am anxious to use it again. You boys come on, go get your pa." They turned tail and left the cook to his business of cooking. (The boys remembered why the cook was at the county farm. The story goes that he had chopped off the head of a man who dared to refuse to back his Model T off a bridge when he was more than halfway across. The head of the Model T's owner had been cut off with a machete knife, then placed on a fence post in the yard of the future cook at the county farm. It was told he sat with a shotgun loaded with buckshot day and night, keeping relatives of the dead man from taking the head to be buried with the body.)

None of the folks in this story regained their smell or taste. No reason was known at that time why such was visited upon these hapless people. Here in the present day very few who have this ailment have yet found relief nor the reason why it is visited on them.

A book I read gave several possible reasons for this problem, said to afflict as many as 2,000,000 Americans. One is "exposure to certain chemicals." This disorder is called anosmia. 🎴

Sack Clothes

He was aged, bent, worked to a frazzle: a tenant farmer. His shirt, however, was snow white across his chest. He would not remove his coat on a hot summer day in 1939; he was on his way to church. He had come to borrow thirty-five cents to put in the plate at the church where he and his family of five granddaughters, along with his crippled wife, went to a big meeting once each summer.

After putting the change in his trembling palm, I asked why he didn't take his coat off and be comfortable as he and the family rode the dusty way in the farm wagon pulled by two matched mules. Slowly he removed his coat and turned around to show me his back. Printed on the sack material his shirt was made from was a life-sized bulldog, faded and dim, but the writing was easily read: "Bull Dog Fertilizer, Best for Your Crops."

With a proud lift of his head he remarked, "I don't mind wearing sack clothes, but I pray every night my granddaughters will be spared having to wear dresses and underwear made from sacks when they are grown. It is bad enough when they are little and all the other folks are wearing the same." He went on to say that he and his wife had bought very few sacks of fertilizer the past summer and sacks were scarce around their house. His wife spoke up, saying, "I wish I could get some printed chicken feed sacks to make the girls school dresses. I'll pay ten cents each, or I can bring citron melons to swap out for the sacks."

Having been brought up to wear flour sack bloomers (bleached and boasting of hairpin lace or tatting), I had never felt shame because most of my relatives and friends also had the same kind of underwear.

I recall today how I longed to get "big enough" to have a button at the end of the band holding up my drawers in place of the draw-string. Mama thought that tying a good bow was the safest method. I might miss the buttonhole or the button might pop off and then where would I be?—with the unmentionables down around my ankles as we played devil-in-the-ditch or other running games at school.

Before I got old enough to be trusted with a button band on my underware, times had picked up enough for me to have elastic in the waist band. Within a few years people quit making shirts, underwear, sheets, towels, pillowslips, bedspreads, and curtains from feed, flour and fertilizer sacks. 🔲

Building a New Barn

I recall the pleasure my brother and I had when our father built a new barn many years ago.

How well I remember two carpenters building the big barn. They were in no hurry, for gathering time was months away and the only contract was a handshake and a promise that the last nail would be in place when the first load of hay was ready for the lofts.

Often when the lumber was used up, the carpenters would go to the pasture, catch two mules, hitch them to a wagon, and go to the upper place, where lumber was stacked after being sawed at the ground-hog saw mill.

They lazed away the days, and we enjoyed the project to the fullest; the many interesting blocks of wood, long thin strips of wood, delightful twisted curls of wood, and lovely piles of fragrant sawdust, which I garnered against a day I was sure I would find a special use for the slightly golden dust. Brother and I played in the barn, swinging from rafters high above the ground. We clambered about like monkeys while Mama threw her arms up and implored us to be careful.

The carpenters had no thought of bringing dinner. Mama seemed to enjoy cooking for extra help, and they appreciated her apple pies, chicken dumplings, and pots of speckled butter beans made tasty with ham bones.

One of the men had a great sweeping moustache and always folded it back neatly when he drank clabber. He was past master at spearing a baked potato with his fork and could peel it with his pocket knife while he balanced it on the three-tined fork.

He didn't think too much of Mama's silverware. He would bring out a leather case and remove his folding fork and knife, a darling teaspoon hinged in the middle, and a real ivory toothpick he placed beside his plate to use if needed. I longed for such a set of eating utensils and prayed that Santa would bring me a set in steel and horn. With those and the folding drinking cup I had tucked away, I thought I would be ready for any event that included eating.

When the barn was ready for roofing, the boards were rived by an old man and his two sons from down near Berwick. They brought iron froes and heavy wooden mallets for this work. Brother and I had the job of stacking the boards in pens about waist high; when nosey hens came around, we would put them in the pens. At dusk dark Mama reminded us to take the hens out. How they would scurry for the hen house in the early dusk.

The carpenters lazed around so long Daddy and his help were bringing up loads of corn before the crib doors were nailed on. The harness room was completed with saddle rack, and many forked tree limbs were nailed upright for hanging harness and mule collars.

In these modern times children never get to know the joy of being around a building project. The carpenters work lickety-split trying to finish so they can start another row of houses, and there are people waiting to move in before the paint is dry.

This past Christmas I went to a building project to ask for some blocks for a visiting child. The manager looked at me with amazement and said, "Lady, lumber costs too much in these times to waste any. I figure to the last inch." I well remember holding on to the end of a rafter while Mr. Bracey sawed away with a hand saw. When I pressed down too hard and the rafter split, it mattered not at all, as there were plenty more from the pile under a pecan tree.

The Pleasures
of Watermelon Cuttings

Do you remember having watermelon cuttings in your salad days? This get-together was the same as a cocktail party in current times only without the hard stuff (however, looking back, I do recall a few men sneaking to the barn to take a little sip from a fruit jar stashed in the corn crib).

Grandpa Causey always had a big cutting during the month of July or August for kith and kin, neighbors, or just anyone who hankered after slices of melon from the largest ones around. Company would gather under tall hickory trees in the side yard where three long benches had been placed with papers spread over them to catch seeds for the chickens.

We children gathered near the tall chimney where we nibbled on four o'clock leaves and sniffed white ginger lilies. Grandpa brought melon after melon from under the high back porch. Grandma busied herself bringing out the huge butcher knife to slice the melons, square salt cellers, and bone-handled knives for grown folks.

Grandpa knew his melons were ripe. The thrill of watching for the red heart to show was almost more than we could stand. First the melon would be turned so the white side was up; next it would be decided that the melon would steady better turned over. This done, the wicked-looking big knife was stuck to the hilt at the stem end and brought with sure steady hand to blossom end. This was done carefully so the melon would not "bust open" when being sliced.

Each melon would be cut in eight slices, and guests were expected to eat down to the rind. This was a job as the melons often tipped the scales at forty pounds or more. Never has there been such pure pleasure as taking one of the bone-handled knives and cutting the heart from the slice, then heaping salt on the tip of the knife and with steady hand sprinkling salt from one tapering end to the other.

Seeds were squirted at courting couples who took our foolishness with good grace. How thrilled we were to see a well-aimed seed land on cheek or chin of those singled out for this form of horseplay.

After our fill of melon, we had the happy chore of taking the rinds to the hogs, pastured and in pen. The pasture hogs were long and mean. We had to watch our toes as we climbed on the rail fence to toss the rinds over. Some of the hogs had curved tusks and weren't above trying to slip one tusk through the spaces between the rails in hopes of drawing blood from a hapless victim.

The pen hogs were of another stripe. After a few months in the pen, they had lost all likeness to the wild lean fellows they once had been. Fattened up, they came to meet us with bellies dragging in the deep mud. Their eyes were mere slits in fat faces and their backs were square with fat. Some were so fat they only got up to eat. Since a melon rind was considered a tidbit, they managed to get their share even if it meant a fight.

When it came time for the company to go home, Grandpa invited every man present to take a melon. It mattered not that melons were piled high on front porches at their houses, and that they were sick of Tom Watsons or Dixie Queens. They meekly took the melon offered by "Cousin Davis," and tucked it under the seat of the buggy or wagon.

Such were the honest, delightful pleasures of a watermelon cutting back when my salad days had only been dreamed about. 🈂

How to
"Pull a Miss Demp"

Whenever Grandmother Budd was confronted with a problem that seemed to have no solution in sight, she often asked her unmarried daughter, Phleta, what to do. Not once can I recall Auntie telling her mother what to do. She would say, "Mama, why don't you 'pull a Miss Demp' on that?" It never crossed my mind to ask who Miss Demp was or what she had done to earn such a lasting impression on my aunt and her mother.

As I grew older, I noticed that many people on Shady Rest used "Miss Demp" to take care of unfinished chores. Questions nobody wanted to answer got this reply: "If you live long enough maybe 'Miss Demp' will tell you."

Once my mother grew vexed as she tried to remove a hemline mark from my summer-before-last best dress, a dress that came to mid-kneecap on my fat legs, stuck out in the back, and was entirely too short, so Mama said. Nothing she tried erased the line. Mama rolled the dress into a bundle, then stuck it in the bureau drawer, saying, "Well, I guess 'Miss Demp' will settle that."

The next morning I questioned Grandmother Budd about Miss Demp. This is the story she told me.

Miss Dempariste Collins was the neighborhood busybody in a nice, kind, helpful way. If there were hogs to be killed, lard to be rendered, chitterlings to be turned and scraped, broomstraw to wring and make into brooms, fertilizer sacks to be sorted, washed, and bleached, or a storeroom put to rights, people would send for Miss Demp. She would come to help. However, if something more interesting came along, it didn't bother Miss Demp one bit to stop working, announcing to one and all, "Now, you leave my 'piddling' alone as I will be back another day." Off she would go, leaving dismayed women with unwanted tasks to be finished.

That, so said my grandmother, was the way the saying "Pull a Miss Demp" got started.

When old man Lisha Spurgeon and his wife were down sick, with nary a chick nor child to tend them, Miss Demp was sent for. She came and stayed until Mrs. Spurgeon was laid in her grave (with room to spare beside her for Mr. S.), then on and on for several years. Back then, neighbors tended to other folks' business and insisted that Miss Demp leave the Spurgeon house or get Mr. S. to marry her.

Miss Demp was all for the idea of getting married except for one thing: she told my grandmother she didn't want to marry a man she had never seen without his hat. This hat was an old brown affair with a rattlesnake band and had seen better days. According to Grandmother, she told Miss Demp that she had known Mr. S. for forty-five years and had never seen him without a hat—summer, winter, in church, even at wakes, and, if her eyes served her right, it was the same old brown hat Miss Demp was objecting to. Grandmother advised Miss Demp to marry if she wanted and not let a little thing like wearing a hat to bed bother her.

The wedding took place, and the couple lived together for nine years. When conversations got around to odd things husbands did, Miss Demp would always ask, "Have anybody ever knowed of a man wearing his hat to bed?"

When Mr. Spurgeon died, neighbors who came to "lay him out" removed his hat before washing him for the viewing and funeral.

His hair was such a matted mess he was put in the coffin without his hair being combed. Even Miss Demp couldn't tell if his hair should be parted on the side or in the middle. No one had seen him without his hat, so there was no way to tell which way would make him look "natural."

All the mourners kept remarking how Mr. S. didn't look like himself. Finally Miss Demp took a hand in the discussion. She brought in his old brown felt hat, raised her husband's head, put the hat on, pulled it to the position where he had always worn it, and then let him down saying, "Anything that can't be solved, hide it or cover it up." Yes, indeed, Miss Demp fixed her husband just right. 🈴

Apple-Drying Time

In mid-October my Grandmother Budd would have boxes of dried apples, stone crocks of apple butter, and jars and jars of apple jelly made and ready for winter eating. Preparing the apples was a chore enjoyed by all.

There were many willing hands to help, as well as plenty of apples from trees on Shady Rest or bought from peddlers who came by in wagons or carts with apples to sell or barter for things they wanted or needed. Those who came to help with the peeling brought their own chairs and knives. It was a gay happy time as several people sat in a circle under the wide spreading limbs of a pecan tree in the back yard.

Grandmother inspected each apple. The perfect ones were cored and handed to a waiting worker who peeled around each end; the apple was then handed to another worker standing at the chopping block. The block was covered with a clean white cloth. After many apples had been sliced in rings, the corners of the cloth were put together and the bundle carried to the back porch, where Aunt Phleta and a neighbor took time from cooking a big dinner (all workers stayed for dinner) to string the apple rings on long strips of unbleached domestic cloth.

A corner of the garden had been cleaned of grass, and pinestraw had been piled about a foot deep to keep down dust. Cheesecloth was hung from the top of the picket fence to the ground to keep yard dust from blowing on the drying apples. Strong wires had been nailed from corner to corner, out about five feet. The strings of apples were laid across these wires, allowing sags and droops to hang down, the better to dry apples in the hot October sun that seemed to fall just right in that special garden corner.

Early mornings saw the sun golding the apples, as Grandmother was up well before dawn to remove the brown paper covering that had kept night moisture off the apples. Later in the morning, yellow jackets and wasps buzzed about, sipping the dripping juices.

Once Grandpa tried to rig up a contraption to collect the juice to feed his little pigs. This proved to be such a mess and of such little value that Grandmother put her foot down, saying that the peelings and cores would be fed to the pigs and that the family would do without "the first fruit jelly."

Late afternoon was time for someone to stand and fan, fan, fan with strips of newspapers slipped into slits cut in cane fishing poles to keep gnats from the apples. These necessary wavers, made by the children during lazy summer days as a fun thing, were stored behind the dining room door until needed.

Once the apples were dried to suit Grandmother, the apple strings were brought inside to be hung in the attic to finish off drying. There they turned into dark brown rings of leather.   Wooden boxes were brought out, scrubbed with hot water and lye soap, rinsed and rinsed, allowed to dry in hot sun, and lined with brown wrapping paper. The apple rings were removed from the strings and packed one layer at a time with paper between the layers. When a box was filled, the wooden lid would be nailed down and the box wrapped in brown paper with the seams and ends sealed with flour paste against bugs and other insects.

On cold winter days a box of apples would be opened and enough apples to make whatever Grandmother planned to prepare would be put to soak, to swell, and to smell of early autumn. One could remember blue skies, golden butterflies, puffy clouds, and clear bright days when cotton was beginning to open.

Grandmother made open-faced as well as two-crusted apple pies, sweetened with brown sugar or molasses, dressed with spices and just-churned butter. These pies would be a special treat served hot with buttermilk. Seconds were almost a must! A cold apple pie on the second shelf of the back porch pie safe was insurance against hunger pains any time of day. 🈁

Old Home Remedies

O ne day last week as I walked through the small woods below the bird dog pens, I spied a huge "devil's snuff box" of meringue color, dotted with pinpoint specks of black. Walking closer, I lightly toed the puffball. At once a cloud of brown smoke billowed from it.

Looking around, I saw several dozen egg-sized ones, thickly clustered on a rotten log. This reminded me of my childhood days when Grandmother Budd gave Brother and me the task of gathering, very gently, several dozen snuff boxes to be stored in glass Mason jars against the time someone on the farm or in the neighborhood might be cut, slashed, or injured in some way, so that the skin would be opened and blood flowing freely.

Treasured for their styptic quality, a puffball would be squeezed over the wound. The brown smoke would settle, and in a matter of minutes (most of the time) the bleeding would begin to lessen.

Grandfather was all for using spider webs, for they could be found in handy places: under the house eves, under the house proper, inside the corn cribs or stables (people back then didn't realize spider webs from the horse barn could have been the cause of lockjaw). The insides of fireplaces that were covered for the summer afforded a steady supply of webs, and in a pinch, scroungy ones could be found in cedar trees.

Once the middle child of Ed and Marida Jackson and I were running fleet-footed across the pasture seeing who could first reach the beech log across Agnes Branch that was used for a foot log.

Carrie, ahead, leaped high in the air and came down on a stick poking up in the ground. It went in the arch of her left foot and came out the side under the ankle bone. There she had to stay until her sister could run screaming and calling to the cotton field a distance away to get Carrie's father.

As I write this, I can recall exactly how the air felt and the sky looked. "Skeeter hawks" came and lit on Carrie's plaited hair. So still and scared were we that we didn't move when a black snake crawled across a ditch just a few steps away.

I broke sweet gum limbs to cover her staked-to-the-ground foot so she wouldn't see the blood seeping around the sharp pointed stick thrust at least two inches beyond her ankle bone. I grew faintly ill watching the bright red blood river down her brown skin to flush and spread in dust-covered blobs. Ants came as if to a picnic, feasting on the warm rich blood, feeling it with their feet and rushing away exactly like their name, racehorse, to bring more of their clan.

Carrie and I waited, growing hotter under the two o'clock sun. A kingfisher flew over, making a harsh cry; he wheeled in mid-air and perched on a dead willow stump. I remember his steady stare, the yellow ring around the black eye; the bottom lid would come up to hood his gaze, and only then would I let out my breath.

When Carrie's father came, he pulled the stick from her foot, and the horrendous damage could then be seen. Where the blood had seeped and dribbled, it now spurted over his hands as he tried to shut off the bleeding by pressing on both openings in the foot. He was crying for spider webs.

Quickly I ran to a scrubby tree and raked a huge bunch of bagworm webs (filled to capacity with worms) and offered the webs to the frantic father. He directed me to bring more, more, and still more until Carrie's foot was swathed in smoky grey, turning the webs red. It was alive with worms trying to escape. Carrie had been quiet and good as gold until she spied the worms—then she set up a howl which was heard at her grandmother's house across the field. Her father carried her home where a good dousing with coal oil killed the worms as well as germs, so said Carrie's mother.

Soaking in warm water with Epsom salts several times a day helped cure Carrie's foot. She was given the best of farm fare to keep up her strength and at the end of five weeks Carrie was once again winning nine out of ten hopscotch games from me.

An amusing note: there were twelve children under ten years of age living on Shady Rest at that time. We saw the difference in treatment given Carrie when she began to walk using a forked oak tree limb for a crutch. We decided to have crutches too. We were a sight, hobbling along trying to get out of chores allotted to us. Our mothers put up with this foolishness for one full day and then the law was laid down, as were the crutches, which were used around the wash pot as firewood to boil green peanuts. 🔳

Gizzard Gems

B rother and I had many collections in the years before our teen days: squirrel tails, rocks, box turtle shells, rattlesnake tail buttons—anything that could be put in a box and then shoved under a bed. We did our best to get all we could of the things we were searching for. The collection which afforded us the most pleasure (and brought in not one penny) was "gizzard gems." For two years in our spare time, we ranged far and wide over the community asking housewives to please save pieces of colored glass found in the gizzards of chickens and other farm fowl killed for the table.

When housewives broke plates and other dishes, these pieces were saved until a box was filled. On a rainy day, children were sent to the chopping block where these pieces of white dishes, as well as colored-glass dishes, would be pounded into small pieces and fed to the chickens in the hopes of making egg shells thicker. Once the hens, turkeys, ducks, or geese gobbled them, these pieces got into the gizzards and underwent steady grinding and polishing. Most housewives had a little shelf over the place where the picking and cleaning of the fowls was done. On the shelf would be placed the bits of colored glass, pretty and wanted. The neighbors were agreeable to giving us the pieces on hand and promised to save all future gizzard gems.

We put the lovely small pieces (about the size of a field pea) of colored glass—red, yellow, green, blue, clear and sometime purple—in Bull Durham tobacco sacks, the kind with yellow drawstrings. These sacks were carefully hidden in secret places.

Rainy days were best for bringing out these hoarded, straight-from-the-gizzard gems to be counted and put in rows according to color and size. Brother and I had the "jump" on the neighborhood children for about three months. Alas, when the word got out, our friends began hounding their mothers to "give us the colored glass from our chickens' gizzards." That broke our little fun thing up.

Our New Orleans aunt, Doll, was visiting Grandmother Budd. Trying to be helpful, she offered to throw corn to the barnyard fowl for their late afternoon feeding. There were fifty or more chickens, thirty turkeys, several dozen ducks, a few geese, and a pea fowl. After flinging the corn, Aunt Doll discovered the diamond in her engagement ring was gone.

It was a nice stone that had been passed down in the Fargot family. Aunt Doll cried and took on so that Grandmother was persuaded to shut all the fowl in the hen house and remove those roosting in trees from their roosts and shut them in the barn hallway. Grandmother promised that when morning came the fowl would be killed one at a time until the diamond was discovered.

Once Uncle Burrel Taylor heard this, as he called it, "pack of foolishness," he offered a simple answer to the diamond recovery. If he was given full range of the diamond operation (no pun intended), he and his wife and three grandchildren would start at once cutting open the craws of the fowl, one at a time. He promised that if the diamond had been eaten, he would find it among the corn in the fowl's craw.

Uncle Burrel, Aunt Lue and the children came and got to work. A chicken would be held by Aunt Lue, Uncle Burrel would gently slice open the craw, empty the contents into his palm, search for the diamond, and return corn to craw. Aunt Lue, using a needle and white sewing thread, would sew the craw together, making a nice trim seam.

Many hens later, they tried the biggest and meanest rooster. There was the diamond. The rooster was so mean and rough, and his spurs so long, sharp, and curved that he slashed his way free, leaving the operators bloody but pleased with themselves. It was three days before the rooster could be rounded up and his craw mended.

Brother and I lost interest in gizzard gems. Spring was knocking around Shady Rest, and we set about searching for gnat balls and oak galls. ▨

When Doors Stayed Open

B ack in my pre-salad days when I believed in the Easter bunny,
Santa, the stork, and the tooth fairy, there was little or no steal-
ing going on where we lived, except for a watermelon or two taken
by pranking boys (who more than likely had bigger melons at home),
a mess of roasting ears by passersby who thought nothing of helping themselves if the patch was beside the road, a chicken lifted
from a limb in the night, or honey taken from a bee tree already
marked (often times on another place), if the tree robbers were drinking home brew or dew from a hidden still. Many of the honey culprits
would be stung from top to bottom, so that their guilt was known
to both the owner of the tree and the community. Of course these
fellows would not be reported to the law, just left alone after the
honey was brought to the owner of the tree.

It was also tempting to "borrow" a few stalks of sugar cane from
someone whose patch was beside a public road. Once when Mama
had taken us to a mill over toward the Jerusalem quarters for a Saturday afternoon outing, we heard the owner of the cane mill talking
to a group of boys about fifteen to seventeen years of age who had
asked for stalks of cane. "No, you got your share night before last
when you went in my patch." When the boys protested, he said,
"I was up in the sweet gum tree by the old lake when all of you
went in, every last one of you. Where is Riger? I saw him with all
of you."

Can you believe country people never locked their doors when
they left home? I remember going to some of these homes with
Marianna for a visit, to swap a "setting of eggs," or to beg for a
special flower cutting or perhaps a few strands of sewing thread,
or to take a mess of fresh vegetables to the ones we were visiting
if they were old or sick. Back then when someone left home for
the spring down the hill to get a bucket of water or to remove buttermilk put there to stay fresh deep down in the water in a heavy
stone jug, or to sit and visit with neighbors, or help deliver a baby,
or to gather firewood, there was no dread of their household things
being stolen. These homes were off the big road (which meant the
mail rider didn't pass this way), down a twisty dirt track where these
roads often ended at the edge of a field, creek, or woods.

When someone had to be away from the house for a matter of
a few minutes or all day, nothing was done to secure the house ex-

cept to put a straw broom across the doorway. If the broom was propped across the door, a-body knew the homeowner would be back in a short spell. If the broom was flat on the floor, yet across the door, the caller should go on home, for the person living in the house would be gone quite some time, at least until dusk dark. Marianna and I would no more have thought of going inside and helping ourselves to things not ours than of trying to fly to the moon.

It is true that we might have gone to the well and drawn a bucket of water to refresh ourselves, or to the spring or branch to sip from a gourd dipper, taking care to hang the gourd another way to let the owner know someone had been there.

If there were chairs or benches in the yard we would rest if tired. If there were no seats we would hunker down in the shade of the house for a few minutes to get our breath for the walk home. Enter the house or porch? Indeed not.

Nowadays most people have two or more locks on our doors, broom sticks to keep glass doors from being opened, and nails in holes over our windows, all in hopes of keeping thieves out. Others have their own secret ways to keep their houses safe and secure.

We had a neighbor two roads over who was cooking outside, using a fancy smoker three sections deep. There was a ham on one shelf and sausage, pork chops and rabbit on another. His wife had made a big pan of dressing for the top shelf. They went to the store for barbecue sauce. Gone only twenty minutes, they returned to find that the smoker was gone with food still cooking. The thieves even took the bag of charcoal and, to add insult to injury, the best coon dog in the county. 🖼

A Privy
on Every Farm

M any years ago outdoor toilets were all the rage (had to be, there was nothing else out in the country). These ranged from snug shelters complete with moons and stars sawed into the doors to a few planks slanted from a low-growing tree limb with the opening facing away from the house or road. Some people stuck four poles in the ground and wrapped them with fertilizer or bailing sacks that were split up the middle so as to allow entrance as needed. Families who "didn't give a hoot" would thrust a pine pole across a fence corner and call it a sanitary toilet.

About the time Mrs. Frances Perkins (who was the first woman cabinet member in the United States and served as secretary of labor under President Franklin D. Roosevelt from 1933 to 1945) riled many from the South with statements about the barefooted population and hookworm, the federal government began sending WPA workers into Mississippi to urge every farm family to have a pit privy. I remember the howls of wrath and threats made against these hapless WPA men who were trying to make a few dollars to feed their families. (The uproar was almost as loud as the one against those who wanted to force farmers to dip their cattle. Thank goodness there was no bloodshed over these privies as there was over cattle dipping.)

Farmers were poor but proud and didn't want the federal government telling them what to do about their private lives. Many were starving and pride was about the only thing they had left.

My father, Hiram Budd, was one of these farmers who didn't want the federal government telling him that his well-built open privies weren't suitable for his family. He decided to go along with the WPA plan after Mama said many other families might refuse also, if he didn't give in.

One federal worker, a handsome young man from a state far away, had a quota to fill—so many toilets to build before he would be finished and allowed to shake the mud of Amite County from his feet and return to his home state. He was invited to do that very thing by every family he visited!

This young man kept after my father to get on with the project. My father wanted three toilets on his farm, and even though this was highly irregular, the WPA worker said he would go along with it since it would fill his quota. At one time the young man hoped to finish and be with his family at Easter to take part in the Easter egg hunt his church sponsored each year.

Local WPA labor was hired to do the pit digging as well as to build the toilets. I seem to remember that the government footed the bill for the lumber, but perhaps I am wrong. My father kept putting off the starting; the days became mild, crops were ready to be planted, and still the three promised little buildings were not finished.

The young man had been told he wasn't welcome on the farm, and if he did come back he better not open his mouth to utter the word "privy." One day he came to the farm and was made welcome, but he was told he would be handled roughly if he mentioned the subject he had been harping on for weeks and weeks. The federal worker assured my father that he wouldn't open his mouth about "you know what"—that he had dropped by because he was lonesome and just wanted to visit.

About that time a heavy rain started and lasted for hours. The visitor was invited to eat dinner. Eating and drinking buttermilk along with blackberry acid and many farm fare dishes, we lingered long at the table until the blackberry pie was dished up and made even more delicious with pouring cream.

Our whole family went to the front porch to talk. As the afternoon wore on, the visitor became desperate and finally leaned over to my father, saying softly, "I need to go to your privy." At once my father jumped up, took the hapless man by his coat collar and seat of his pants and sort of "dog-trotted" him off the porch, up the walk, out the front gate, across the stomp, and then to his car, which was stuck hub deep in mud.

A new WPA man came who agreed with my father that "this privy deal" was about the craziest thing he had ever heard. Once my father had someone to agree with him, the finishing up was done within one week. Husband, wife, and children had their own cozy pit privies painted red with a stain said to last a lifetime.

A footnote: years later a man came to visit the Budd family. He was a son of the first WPA man in our life. He stayed three days. How we loved hashing over old times with him. It seemed that his father remembered the Budd family fondly. 🔲

A Shivaree

I looked forward to the day when plowing in the west forty would be done. Ben and Annie, who lived on our farm, were going to marry that very weekend. Already their snug house stood among whispering pines at the edge of the upper place. The house was brand new with a blue front door and a nice porch with solid heart-pine steps dripping with globs of rosin.

Came the last day in April, and things shaped up so the wedding could take place. We stripped the yard and even ventured into the graveyard for roses and lilies to deck the house of the to-be-wedded couple. Annie had everything new in the way of wedding clothes, bought in Gloster at Max Kohn's store. Ben was quite proud of the first suit he had owned, ordered from Sears, Roebuck and Co.

Mama and many of those living in and around Shady Rest had baked pies and cakes for several days: layer, stack, pound and even a few sad ones. Pies were open-face, criss-cross crust, covered, and deep-dish cobblers.

Chicken pies were made in dish pans to be baked hours before the wedding. A great array of pickles, relishes, and dessert peaches had been given as gifts, name tags attached. These would be served, as would a freezer of ice cream, if the ice truck man was on time. All guests had been asked to bring their own cup and spoon to enjoy the ice cream. No flat saucers allowed!

Cousin Zack came on his white mule to preside over the wedding and pronounce the couple man and wife.

Annie's mother snubbed and sniffed the whole time, knowing she would now have to get up and start doing for herself. Annie had been the one to cook and bottle-wash for the past fifteen years.

After the wedding and feast, Mama and Daddy went over to Liberty to a meeting, leaving Brother and me with Uncle Jack and his wife Marianna. No sooner had they turned the curve above the pine forest than Marianna broke the good news to us that she was going to take us to the shivaree at the newly wedded couple's house that night.

About seven we began to get ready. I hunted around and found my old tambourine. Brother was going to take a little pig to pull its tail and make it squeal, and Uncle Jack took the old copper pickle kettle and the clapper from the big outside dinner bell to bang the kettle. Marianna took a tin dishpan and a cook spoon to make noise. As we went out the door, she handed me my great-grandmother's brass dinner bell to ring, as the tambourine had too many little tinkle pieces missing.

As we went down the road to the newlyweds' house, whole families joined us. Uncle Simon Pipkin brought along his fiddle with only two strings; he couldn't play a note but he made awful screeches and noises. Big Blue Bill brought three dogs and a strong stick to beat them with so they would howl to the warm night sky. Fellow Cain rode his performing mule, to the delight of the children who enjoyed seeing the mule walk about on its hind legs and bray on command. He made the night ring with brays and would continue until a special command was given to stop.

We had a wonderful time! We screamed long and loud, calling for Ben and Annie to come out and greet their company and join in the fun. They didn't budge!

Early the next morning, we found to our utter dismay that the house had been empty. Annie's mother cut such a ''rusty'' over having to stay alone that Annie and Ben spent the night with her to calm her down! 🀙

Cousin Cricket
and the Climbing Hog

Cousin Cricket was known as a stern yet just man. It could never be said that he didn't give the devil his due. Everyone in his neighborhood knew that he asked no favors and expected none, that he gave no quarter in any matter. If someone got him where the hair was short, he looked for no mercy. He stood ready to take his medicine, the same as he would dish out if he were in the other fellow's shoes.

His own mother could do nothing for him, not even knit mittens as presents for his children (her own flesh-and-blood grandchildren); he paid her so much per pair. He charged her board, ten dollars per month, year in and year out, and sometimes she had to go into her saved coins to make out the amount. She was entitled to a small stipend from the pauper board of the county; however, Cricket would not allow her to apply for it.

It is said that every person in the world meets his match, gets what he deserves if he lives long enough. As I live and breathe, we saw Cousin Cricket a whipped man—he who had never asked favor of chick nor child, man nor beast.

Cousin Cricket had the strength of an ox. He ate anything and everything grown on his farm and digested it too with no trouble. Never did he have to stick a finger in the soda jar to settle his stomach or ease indigestion pangs from overindulgence. He ate just so much and no more.

True he wasn't stingy like Cousin Flea, his brother (so nicknamed because he jumped from one thing to another), who was said to be so tight he took the tires off his Model T after each trip to town and hung them up so they would last longer. When starters were invented on cars, he had his sons push off the car so as to make the starter last longer. He never tooted the car horn for fear of wearing it out.

When I was quite small, I truly believed Cousin Flea walked across you-know-where backward trying to catch a flea so he could skin it, save the tallow, and nail its hide on the barn wall. Once, in all good faith, I asked him how many flea hides it took to make a pair of shoes. He questioned me closely, until in tears I told him what his folks and neighbors said about him.

Cousin Cricket was cut from a different bolt of cloth if I could believe my elders, especially a maiden cousin who spent her days visiting from one family to another helping out, as unmarried women did in those days. Whenever our cousin stayed at Cricket's, she helped Cricket's wife put up tomatoes, catsup, pear relish, muscadine butter, cabbage kraut, and dried, canned, and sauced apples from many trees. After this work was over, Cricket handed her so much cash for her work and then asked for a set amount for board. She was always so mad it took Mama the better part of the two weeks allotted to our family to soothe Cousin's feathers. She often vowed and declared that if Lella wasn't her double first cousin, she would never set foot in that Cricket's house again.

Years passed, and the Cricket children married and moved away; some went out west, others to big towns. With no children to help out, Cricket was not asking for favors nor granting them.

One day a letter came from Dorsey, his oldest daughter, saying she was sending her sons (triplets), age fifteen, to visit, and would Papa meet the train in Gloster—come in the double buggy as she was sending her mama some kitchen things.

The boys, Ronald, Donald and Conald, were Cousin Cricket over and over—they looked like him, acted as he did, and walked the same, a sort of slide shuffle. Three cowlicks stood up in the crowns of their heads, nine in all. Tell them apart? Nobody could! It made no difference, Grandmother Budd said. Each was sassy and bad as the other. They went around en masse doing tricks to upset their grandpa as well as the neighbors.

Things rocked along for three weeks. Then trouble began over at Hard Scramble, Cousin Cricket's lush farm. Seems as if he had ordered off for a fine boar hog and put it into a peeled pine pole pen. The next morning the hog was gone—climbed right over the fence, so said Cousin Cricket. He and the triplets went to the woods where they found the hog rooting, pretty as you please. They cut four pine poles to build the pen higher, but the next morning they found the same thing—the hog was gone. He had climbed out, leaving marks to prove it right on the poles.

The pen grew fifteen feet high with boards laid over the top, but it made no difference. The boards were nosed off, and the hog was gone to the creek bottom to look for tender roots. Lots of beech mast still on the ground was dessert for him. The pen grew even taller, so much so that the last four poles were double notched, but it made no difference. The hog was gone by daylight. He was some climber to make eighteen feet.

Finally Cousin Cricket came asking for the first favor in his life from my grandfather. He wanted Grandfather to stand watch and see how the hog managed to get out of the pen. He had stood watch two nights, but the hog was smart, and when he was being watched he knew it and stayed in the pen, nice as pie.

Grandpa came to the little woods where the pen was built, well after dusk, and climbed into a tall oak tree to wait. He had told Grandmother he was going coon hunting. As the moon rose, he saw the triplets, Donald, Ronald, and Conald, creeping to the hog pen. The three lifted one corner high enough to let the hog out, and then using brush tops they whisked their footprints away.

Grandpa didn't have the heart to tell Cousin Cricket what had happened, so he pretended to have dropped off for a catnap, only to wake and see Mr. Hog hotfooting it toward the branch. Grandmother called long distance to tell Dorsey the triplets were fretting her pa, and they would be coming home the next day.

Cousin Cricket and the triplets cut more poles to build the pen twenty feet high. They put a slop chute into the trough and placed planks at a slant around the sides at the top of the pen. Of course no hog in the world could climb up twenty feet and get over slanted boards—fifteen feet, eighteen feet had been mastered but twenty feet never!

Cousin Cricket did not learn of the trick his grandchildren played him, and to my knowledge he never asked for another favor. The most he did was speak to his old mule in a stern voice, saying, "Gita-up," flapping the worn rope reins, and that really wasn't a favor, since a mule was supposed to "git-a-up" when ordered so! 🐾

Raoul

It was a hot day in July when the telegram came saying that the wife of a distant cousin was coming for a visit and, best of all, was bringing her son, Raoul.

The distant cousin had gone to France on his twenty-first birthday. He had been given the trip as a present from his papa and also as a bribe to settle down in the Delta and farm, only it didn't work out that way. He met, fell in love with, and married a French girl the first week he was in Paris. As the happy couple sailed homeward, the cousin sickened, died, and was buried at sea. The bride came to the Delta, lived there about sixteen months, and then returned to France with her young son.

We had never seen the French bride, or the son, Raoul, who was now nine years old; however, we felt as if we knew them from letters that came to Grandmother Budd from her cousin Blanche (grandmother of Raoul). The letters said he was a prince, blond and beautiful, even if he was a boy.

Now the foreign relatives were coming to Shady Rest for a visit. The next morning when we went over to Grandmother's, the French cousins were there.

Nanette was all we expected—tiny and dark, she talked with her hands, shoulders and eyes. She used words that we couldn't understand. Her waist was nineteen inches and my big toe would have fit her size-three shoe. Raoul was a runt, with a pinched face and long blond curls that hung to his waist, black velvet pants, and white shirt with big collar and pearl buttons.

A bandage on a skinny leg was explained as covering a furuncle. Nanette told Grandmother that Raoul was troubled with helminthiasis—in other words, he was vermiculated. Medicine from the big bottle on the kitchen table was to be given three times a day, only Raoul wouldn't take it like a reasonable child. So, with a shrug, she said, "Never mind, perhaps he will outgrow this trouble."

We loved Nanette. She was quick, sweet, precious, and lovable. She played games with us all day long, while our mother and aunt did nothing but cook, clean, tend babies, can vegetables, make jelly, wash, iron, and even sew, never coming out to play and swim with us in the blue hole at Waggoner Creek.

Early mornings found Nanette dressed in a peignoir with her long black hair tucked under a mutch. She put the house to rights by having the children beat each feather bed to a towering puff. Often as not, she would fall back in the middle of the bed and invite us to join her in a storytelling time.

Once when Uncle Jack was tending to some rainy-day work, Nanette came to the kitchen and told Grandmother Budd that, honestly, the scythe wasn't properly in its snath and the ax was a disgrace the way the helve was set in.

She would "illumniate" a room, gathering several lamps so we could have plenty of light. She would slice paper-thin strips from a gammon (smoked ham). She would gather quills to make Indian headbands for play. She told us how she suffered an attack of suppurative tonsillitis on the trip from France.

Nanette talked one of our half-grown cousins into catching three hares (in the middle of summer, mind you, when everybody knows rabbits aren't fit to eat and their babies are waiting for mama to come home) and cooked up a stew of pickled rabbits called hasenpfeffer, which was delicious over fluffy rice.

Raoul went around being a clean tidy child, minding his manners, suffering one furuncle after another (they looked just like the boils we had off and on all summer, every summer), and taking his medicine about twice a week. His long blond curls were washed every other day, dampened with sugar water, then wrapped around a polished stick to shape the curls. He was a sight; we teased him until he wept and then ignored him until he wailed, never taking him into our magic circle or inviting him into our secret room under the baled oat straw high in the big barn loft.

He looked as if he wouldn't bleed a drop if you cut off an arm or leg. He picked at his food, cried out in his sleep, and gnashed and ground his teeth, so said Grandmother. She muttered to Auntie that she hoped to get her hands on that child for one week—she would cut his hair and dose him with the right kind of medicine. About helminthiasis, she snorted to anyone who would listen, "I don't know what that means but I do know what is wrong with Raoul."

Nanette went to Natchez to visit for six weeks, leaving Raoul with Grandmother. No sooner had the buggy turned the first bend than Raoul's curls lay on the floor; he cared not one whit for the curls, giving them to me to pin over my own straight snuff-colored hair.

Auntie went to town for five cents worth of vermifuge and a pair of overalls. Sister and I gathered garlic buttons for steeping in hot water for strong garlic tea. A five-day treatment was followed by five skipped days and then another round took place. Mama treated us at the same time, for it was well known that one vermiculated child could infest the whole crowd of children.

After that, Raoul was a different child. He ate like a pig, kicked our shins, climbed the tallest trees, made us say passwords to get into our own secret room under the oat straw. He even sassed Grandmother one day and got a little switching. He got so dirty that new overalls had to be bought, as one pair wasn't enough.

Grandmother knew she had cured Raoul!

When Nanette returned she was amazed at the change in her child. He was strong, fat, brown, and sassy. She said, "Never did medicine take so long to work. He has been taking that tonic for over a year—that is, when he wanted to. It is magic, no?"

Grandmother looked up from her quiltmaking and said, "Your doctor must have been mistaken. There was nothing wrong with Raoul, except that he was wormy." 🈁

Adventures in Photography

When we were small, Mama thought her children were the most beautiful in the world; I know she did, for she had our pictures made every chance she got. The traveling photographer, the fly-by-night studio, camera fan, doting relatives with cameras, and her own trusty little Brownie—Mama was fair game to all.

Whenever Mama had a few dollars saved from her egg and butter money, she would say to Daddy, "I believe I will go to Baton Rouge to see my sister Hallie for a few days." Sewing new dresses for the girls and pants and shirt for our brother was necessary, as Mama didn't want the same clothes to be worn as in the last pictures.

On the morning of the day we left to go to Baton Rouge we were up before dawn. Since we weren't hungry for heavy food, we made do with toasted biscuit and hot cocoa. Sister's hair and mine had been rolled up on kid curlers, so that when it was brushed out the look was that of a freshly unraveled well rope. Marianna, Mama's helper, had made a lunch complete with buttermilk in a quart jar. It was thought the buttermilk would settle our stomachs if we got train sick.

When we reached Baton Rouge, Mama used the telephone to ask prices at various studios; when the proofs were ready, Mama went back to the picture place to bargain for more for her money. Picking out a particular proof was a hard decision, for we were cute (I have the pictures, don't I?), and Mama thought we were beautiful. One time the proofs were especially good, so Mama went to the depot and turned in her return tickets, spending four dollars more on pictures than she had counted on. Daddy was very vexed that he had to crank up the Maxwell and chug all the way to Baton Rouge for his family, but when he saw the pictures, he too was captivated by our cuteness.

I sincerely hope all of Mama's and Daddy's relatives liked pictures. Every Christmas the flat package arrived regularly; there was no wondering what they were getting as a present.

Our New Orleans aunt made pictures when she came to visit. Dogs, cats, horses, mules, and even chickens were fair game for her Brownie. There would be a story behind every snapshot.

We loved the little old man who came by once a year to make

pictures. He had a small wagon pulled by a very small donkey. He made pictures for ten cents, and if you were mounted on the donkey that would be five cents extra. Of course we all wanted to ride while being photographed. Mama, being a bargain hunter, got the old fellow to take a rooster as part payment; within a few days the rooster was back. When the pictures were delivered in about a month, the old man wanted Mama to pay for the barnyard use of the rooster. Mama wanted him to pay for the corn the rooster had eaten. Finally the old fellow knew he was bested so he took the sullen rooster and left. He never came back. Mama said he might have died.

Mr. Tom Costas lived in McComb, where he ran the McColgan Hotel and Cafe. He had a camera that made poscard-size pictures. He made a picture of my sister Rhoda Pearl sitting in a shell box. The brand name showed so plainly that the shell company used the picture for its calendars the next year. We were very proud of our sister. Once we were in Baton Rouge in a resturant, and there on the wall was a calender with Rhoda's picture. We went from table to table telling diners the picture was of our sister—needless to say, not one believed us. Mama was quite chagrined that they couldn't see the resemblance, though by then Sister had grown a full head of hair and gained ten pounds, so the likeness was very slight.

On the back of every picture, Mama wrote what we had on, how old we were, our conditions (colds, mumps, and measles), and the state of the weather. My favorite: Rose Budd sitting on a table, looking into a hand mirror, hair straight as a stick. On the back, Mama wrote, "Rose age four years and three months, weight 50 pounds, weather very rainy, reason for hair being straight. Dress made from one of her aunt Doll's china silk dresses with blue roses appliqued on yoke. Had to switch her to make her behave."

The photographer would slowly lose his happy face as Mama combed our hair, took us to the toilet, and cautioned us to hold up our shoulders, smile, and watch the little birdie. She would even give us crackers if we said we were hungry.

Finally the long-suffering photographer told Mama he knew of a man in New Orleans who made wonderful pictures at half the price he was charging. He gave Mama the address, and the next time Mama got picture fever we went to New Orleans to visit a dear friend. Needless to say, the address was a vacant lot.

Today I love the pictures Mama had made of her children. I have been saving my egg money and have an address of a place in Jackson which makes pictures at half price. I have an idea, however, that the address is a vacant lot; you see, the photographer over McComb way has been given to deep sighs and head shakes when I take time to fluff Rose, Jr.'s hair for the third time. 🔳

Party Line Fever

"You get what you pay for" is a saying that has been around all of my life. I remember a time, however, when the Budd family's party line provided much more entertainment value than the small sum paid out each month to the phone company.

It was a "catch as catch can" affair, with the lines belonging to families on the ten-party phone line. A person wanting service simply ran a wire to the nearest line already connected to "central" at Liberty. In our case, we joined the Smiths, who had a line over hill and dale up a woven wire fence to Hog Eye Branch. They in turn hitched onto the Browns, who by splicing and borrowing wire far and near were able to piece out to the Castons at the crossroads.

We were in a talking fever! We were connected to the outside world five miles away—that is, if one neighbor could be talked into letting the wire stay tied together. When this man became vexed with a neighbor, he simply walked to the end of his porch and cut the wire, leaving the hapless owners beyond him without service.

Our phone hung on the wall, in what we fondly called the parlor, right by the front door so wandering breezes could cool the one doing the talking.

Mama dearly loved the phone; she was a real homebody. She did her visiting via phone, picking the strangest times to talk. She would be ironing with five sadirons next to a big fire in the fireplace. Even after a hot iron was rubbed on cedar branches to give a good smell to the clothes, the iron would still be too hot for the little checkered apron unrolled on the board. While the iron cooled, Mama would get on the phone to chat with a neighbor. When she hung up the phone, the iron would be too cold and the others red hot. While the cool one was heating and the hot ones cooled down, Mama would decide to chat just a minute or so longer. This cycle could go on for an hour or so, until Mama took herself firmly in hand and turned a deaf ear and blind eye to the enticing phone.

The phone box hung so high the children had to stand on a chair to talk into the adjustable mouthpiece. Quite often we would step off the chair and fall to the floor. Having held on to the receiver, we would jerk it loose from the box. After about six months, the once-long cord had been jerked out and repaired so often that it was a problem to hold the receiver to your ear and talk into the mouthpiece at the same time.

Quite often the batteries in the phones would become weak so that those living at the end of the line couldn't reach central. Mama would call the nearest neighbor who would get her neighbor on the other side of her to help, and all three would ring at the same time, thereby causing the operator in Liberty to know that someone in the rural area needed help.

Arrangements were made with the central lady to ring our house several times a day to see if we needed to ring someone in Liberty or beyond. The owner of the phone service had several young girls working for her, and they often forgot to call. We would be hemmed in for days when the real central was sick or visiting. Once after trying for the better part of two days to get central, Daddy sent Uncle Jack, riding horseback, with a note to central to ask Dr. Quin to call Shady Rest. Daddy was under the weather and wanted to ask the doctor if home remedies we had on hand would cure him.

When our aunt Doll was very ill in Little Rock, Shady Rest phone batteries were so worn out it took five neighbors helping to ring central before she would answer. My father asked the people on the line to hang up so he would be able to talk long distance to Arkansas. After he had talked, he rang the first person on the line, which was a signal for all to pick up and listen. They heard the news that his baby sister had died only minutes before his call came in.

Our phone bill was $1.25 per month. We had service (after a fashion) along with all the news up and down Waggoner Creek; we learned secrets told on the party line. Of course our secrets were no longer ours, because the neighbors loved to listen, too.

The Year of
the Great Drought

A lways there was enough food to share, even in the year of the great drought, but there was no water to spare, not even enough to bathe in. Doing without water was awful!

Gardens were planted on suitable packets of land and were watered from deep holes that were only half-filled that summer. It was the year I would turn twelve in November. That summer no berries dotted the powder-dry woods. Cherry and plum trees leafed out at the proper time, only to have their leaves curl and wrinkle before buds formed. Real gardens planted in need of rain to sprout seeds were only humped rows of dirt. Whereas once we worried over spring floods, this year Mama and Daddy searched the skies in hope of rain clouds. Bright hot brassy days of summer passed, and no crops were raised at all. Only stunted fields of sorghum lifted parched leaves in silent supplication to the skies.

All wasn't sear and drear for the children; down on Waggoner Creek there were two blue holes partly filled with water from springs. We swam, dipped water to wash clothes (the house well afforded only enough water to drink), and fished on special events such as a birthday.

All summer long we watched towering pines turn yellow and drop their needles. It was queer to see trees as bare in August as they had been in December. Hogs were lean and long, for the only corn to be had was carried over from the year before, and seed corn must be saved against the next year's planting. There were no nuts for us to gather and of course none for the furry folks in the woods. Birds and wild game died when water holes and wet weather branches dried up, and there was little or no food for them. We made no syrup that year, for the sugar cane didn't get over knee high. Trying to chew the paper-dry stuff was useless.

Finally the well began to give water that was milky and not good to the taste. One cold winter morning the milky water had to be thrown out. Several squirrels, crazed by thirst, managed to fall into the well and perish.

All the drinking water we could depend on was one thin stream that bubbled up in the bottom of a spring down in a deep valley a mile from the house. Daddy and the hired help built a strong fence around the spring, boxing it in with heavy boards and screen over the top to keep frogs and small animals out. The spring purled so slowly that at almost any time of day someone was there getting every precious drop that flowed.

Days dawned cold and hard. We think a cold wet day is something to be endured, but a dry searing cold day in February is something you have to feel to believe. The days were so cold the handle of an ax burned through worn gloves, and the dry wood was so pithy it simply fell apart in chunks. There was no green wood to mix with the dry. Trees had died while standing, and the few living ones must not be cut. They must be saved against the time when rains would come.

(We children were in hog heaven, for there were no baths. We wore our clothes for a week at a time. Saturday night was bath time, and the same water was used to rinse out underwear.)

Ankle-deep dust in fields shifted with the biting north wind. My father talked of moving to town and trying to get a job. One day he came in to tell that the spring had stopped flowing during the night. This meant hauling water for over six miles round trip from Grandfather Causey's deep well.

Daddy pounded fist into hand saying, "I know there is water somewhere on Shady Rest. If only Taylor Weems was around to make a 'dowsing,' and find a well for us." Years before, Taylor had been laughed out of Amite County with his forked stick and belief that he could dowse. It was said that he journeyed to California to help find water there where farmers had just begun to irrigate fields.

The Budd family came up with twenty-five dollars, and a letter went to the last address known for Taylor Weems. We waited to see if one dry day Taylor would come striding down the road, forked stick in hand, and dowse a well for us. As a sinner pins hopes on the coming revival to save him and show the way to heaven, so the Budd family waited for Taylor Weems to come out of the west and find a deep underground stream of water. Surely on the vast farm reaching from the haunted house on the south to the already-dead pine forest to the north, from Uncle Ben's rail fence on the west to the dummy line where the sun came up each morning, somewhere there would be water.

We had faith that if there was water underground, a man could take a forked stick and walk along holding it at just the right angle, and that stick would bend and continue to bend until the ends would bend and quiver, showing where the water was.

That is, if the man was a dowser of the first rank, as was Taylor Weems. Ah! The very name of Weems could send shivers up your back. The Weems family was a large and lusty brood living back in the woods, without the helping hand of a woman. Folks said the Weems men had worked their poor ma to death years before, and now they lived in a scrambled-up house. Cooking was done in the front room in a stone fireplace. Dogs and hogs wandered in and out at will, chickens roosted on the front porch, and hens laid on the unmade beds. A great-aunt of the men told Mama the boys would fling back the covers before crawling into bed, never bothering to look for eggs.

I remember they had a rattle-trap car. How thrilled I was to notice a hen sitting on eggs right on the back seat. The hen rode around the countryside until she hatched; then she brooded her babies until they were old enough to fly over the sides of the touring car. Oh yes, they were fed and watered in the car.

And then Taylor went away, never sending a word home until one day a letter written in a fancy hand came to our box. It asked us to get word to Mr. Weems that his son Taylor had a job in California as a "hydroprestidigitationest." The letter was written by goodness knows who, for none of the Weems family could read or write a word, and it wasn't likely that Taylor had learned to do either in the few years he had been gone.

After the letter was sent to Taylor, we waited and waited, hauling water from Grandfather Causey's deep well, which was flowing strong and crystal clear as it did in the wettest weather.

No longer did the rumble of thunder in the night send the whole family outside to stand shivering in the cold hoping for a sudden patter of raindrops on the tin roof.

Walks to school were no fun, since there were no long icicles hanging from frozen banks, no ice-covered ditches to walk on, no snowflakes falling that teacher could use to make snow ice cream.

One day as we walked to school, we met a man limping down the road. It was Taylor. We turned around and went back home with him. It was one of the most exciting days of my life.

He was never one for small talk and said right away, "Let's get a forked stick." He selected a Y-shaped hickory limb and started walking over the back yard. Nothing happened. The side yards and front yard were dowsed. Nothing happened. Shaking his head, Taylor began walking backward toward the "stomp" (the place in front of a house where wagons, buggies, surreys and, later, cars were parked. The name comes from a host saying to company, "Unhitch your horses and let them stomp around a little.")

Taylor looked at me and with a motion of his head called me to him. Handing me the stick, he showed me how to hold it, palms up almost to my chin. Nothing happened. Then he laid his hands on my wrists, and the stick began to bend. I grasped the forked part tightly. The single end continued to dip, and right there in the middle of the stomp was where the well was dug.

Mama was delighted to have water and fretted not that the well was right in front of the house—that is, until rains came and the dry wells were filled with water. The stomp well was capped when the other wells were in use again.

For weeks we played at dowsing but never again did I get so much as a dip out of the forked stick.

A good many years ago I read an article telling about a Taylor Weems who had passed away in Amboy, California. The article mentioned that Mr. Weems had discovered water in unlikely places over a period of years by a method called "dowsing." The article also stated that he was a past master in the art of hydroprestidigitation.

After almost forty years I knew what kind of work Taylor Weems was doing when his letter came to get his pa word about his job. He was only doing what came naturally to him—water dowsing. 🏮

A Story of Perseverance and Triumph

T he following story was told to me over a period of two years: "My mama and papa were married when she was fifteen and he seventeen. Now, this wedding wasn't a 'jump over a broom stick' affair—they had a regular license. The wedding was held in the home of Mrs. Clark, and hot gingerbread and buttermilk were passed out for refreshments.

"In the next eleven years, nine children were born. I was the oldest. Eight months after my father was killed in a saw mill accident, another baby was born.

"Long before my father died, I was doing little jobs for the neighbors; one I remember well. This neighbor had several milk cows that wouldn't quit eating in the fields (back then, farmers turned their cows out in the cotton and corn fields) and come to the barn to be milked. It was my job to go into the fields and by main force thrash the cows out. This was awful, for the cockleburs were higher than my head and were dry and scratchy. I was scratched until I bled.

"The cows' tails were loaded with burs and must have weighed ten or eleven pounds. It was my other job to hold the cow tails while Mrs. Jones milked, since one of these switching tails could knock her off the milk stool. I helped take the foaming buckets to the milk room where Mrs. Jones would pour skim milk into a ten-pound lard bucket, put the lid on tight, and then strain a five-pound lard bucket of milk for me to take home. These two buckets of milk were my pay and were something we needed and enjoyed.

"Before my daddy died, he had made a two-wheeled cart to pull our little crippled sister about. This cart was used to bring the milk home each night. I had about a mile to go and it was already dark. How I made those wooden wheels turn as I sped toward home and Mama's loving greeting. When I reached the big sweet gum tree just up the road from our house, I would see the front door open and know Mama had heard the cart wheels squeaking, as well as my bare feet pounding the dirt road. How good the flickering fire looked through the open door. I was home!

"As soon as I washed up we had supper. Mama had two big black iron skillets of cornbread ready, crusty on top and bottom with plenty of crumb in the middle. There were not enough bowls to go around, so two children ate from the same bowl. Mama crumbled the bowls full of the still-warm bread and poured skim milk and a full cup of whole milk over the bread. Then we fell to eating. Never do I remember the children fussing over who was getting the most. When we finished our bread and milk, there would be a baked sweet potato for each of us. The potatoes were soft and delicious, having been baked in the fireplace ashes.

"Some nights we would have sweet potatoes mashed in the bowls with sweet milk poured over. For dessert we would have the bread with molasses and drink the skim milk. We didn't have butter often (only when Mama worked away from home and took her pay in butter and white sugar). However, Mama saved every drop of bacon fat. After it hardened, we would spread this smoky delicious goodness over the hot bread and put molasses on top.

"Mama was a great one to try and have chickens. At one time, we had fifteen hens with only a few laying. The little children kept a sharp ear out for the hens' cackle and then scurried about searching for the nests where they had laid. Each spring Mama would do a day's work for a setting of eggs so she could have fryers to cook and eggs for her sweet cooking.

"By this time I was taking a man's place in the fields, and the chore of keeping the hawks away from the far-roaming hens and their biddies was turned over to the small children. Can you imagine children four, five, six and seven years of age being put to such a task in the present day?

"Christmas was not a time of expecting help from outsiders, since other families were as hard pressed to get food and a few clothes for their families as we were. Mama and I did our best for the children using farm food and homemade presents.

"Mama made shuck dolls for the girls. I recall her fretting because she dared not use flour sacks to make dresses for the dolls, since the sacks were needed to make underwear for the children. How clever Mama was to make the dresses from fringed shucks and curled chicken feathers.

"Mama always saved back a sack of peanuts so we could parch them several times during the holidays. What made these peanuts different? When we picked the nuts from the vines in the fall, we saved all the preacher peanuts (three to a shell) in a special sack that was hung from a rafter in the front room to keep rats from getting to them.

"There would be no white sugar at our house to do Christmas baking. When Mama worked for Mr. and Mrs. Jones, she was paid with white sugar, butter, and eggs. We thought this a real blessing. After Mama had baked her syrup cakes in layers, she would make boiled icing using the white sugar and egg whites. The little children would be busy cracking hickory nuts and picking out the meats to be sprinkled between the layers of the cakes. Never even today have I tasted anything so delicious as Mama's white icing cakes!

"One Christmas I love to remember! Wood was piled high in one corner of the room that had been scrubbed with lye soap and white sand. The children were bathed and dressed in ironed every-day clothes. There was no talk of not having Santa gifts. The girls had a perky hair bow each and their shuck dolls. The boys each had three glass marbles. There was a box of wax color crayons to be shared by all and a pair of jump ropes which Mama explained were plow lines to be played with until time to break the garden and field patches. Each child had a new lead pencil with a rubber eraser.

"I had a new ax, which Mr. and Mrs. Jones had bought for me, along with a file to keep it sharp. Best of all I had Mama's pride in me.

"There was a knobby sack under one bed, and when we opened it there were two oranges for each person in our family—something we had never tasted. We were so careful eating them; we held a saucer under the oranges, so that not a drop of juice was wasted.

"The food that Christmas was perfect: two stewed hens, dump-lings and lots of milk gravy, baked sweet potatoes, a nice pat of butter, a dish of canned beans and one of cabbage. The syrup pitcher was filled with new syrup, and there were two big pans of white flour biscuits crusted on top and bottom with lots of crumb inside to soak up the dumpling gravy. Last of all was the icing cake. Each one had a thick slice, and the rest was wrapped in a clean cloth and put in the safe for another day.

"Before bedtime, Mama let us make a measure of pulled molasses candy. It didn't turn out as pretty and white as when Mama made it; however, we had a blessed good time. I remember this being the best Christmas to come my way, even including the years when times were better.

"When Mama and I, along with the three older children, went out to help clear new grounds in the coldest weather, something had to be done with the younger children, as they could not be trusted not to play in the fire. Mama came up with the idea of driv-ing spike nails into the heavy logs that made the walls of the room where the fireplace was. When it was time to go out to work, each child would be put into a heavy tow sack and hung from one of the nails. The nails were just far enough from the floor so the children couldn't stand up and lift the sack from the nail. My sisters and brothers didn't seem to mind being sacked whenever they had to be left alone, but my soul died a little each time I helped Mama hang these little children on the walls. I thanked God I was older and had been spared this.

"Mama was a very clean person. I remember taking these sacks to a small stream below our house where I washed them and hung them on bushes to dry. This was necessary because the children were often left for long hours and had to relieve themselves in the sack.

"We never left the children without something to eat. They were forced to eat a good breakfast, and the baked potato or corn pone for their lunch was placed beside them in the sack.

"We would build up a good fire, hoping it would last until dinner time when Mama would walk home and build up the fire. Sometimes we were too far away to to do this, and the room became bitter cold. The children seemed to go into a sort of coma. It hurt when we arrived to find a cold house and to see that when the children were taken from the sacks, they lay on the floor in the same cramped position they had been in in the sacks.

"Summertime was another story—the children had a happy, gay time picking berries, tending to the chickens, and playing with kittens. However, they had to be kept from the branch, where deep holes were temptations to unwatched children who loved to play in water. We built a sizable pine pole pen, roofed over with closely laid poles and discarded lumber from an old barn. There was a shelf where naps could be taken, a bucket of water, gourd dipper, and a potty of sorts in one corner. The children had old magazines they could look at and tin cans and old dishes to play house with. They enjoyed their playhouse and on Sunday afternoons when neighbor children came to visit they too enjoyed playing there.

"I want to be quick to point out that Mama and I were not abusing the little ones. I recall other children falling in the fire and being burned or drowning in the creek or branch. We were doing the best we could.

"I continued working for the Jones folks when they needed me. One day the summer I turned thirteen, Mrs. Jones showed me a book, then told me she was going to teach me to read (I had never been to school). The book was a Baby Ray primer. At once I realized that some of the funny-shaped things in the book were exactly like things on the walls of our house. (Mama and I used pages torn from old Sears catalogues and newspapers to paste over cracks in our walls.) I didn't know what the shapes were, but I recognized them as old friends seen for all the days of my life in daylight and flickering firelight on the walls of our home. I am not bragging when I say I could soon read the words even when the pictures were covered.

"The year I was fourteen, Mr. Jones became bedridden. They hired me to work full time, since Mrs. Jones was a frail woman and could not turn her husband in the bed. I was able to do the turning for her. Mr. Jones didn't want his wife out of his sight, so the barn-yard work all fell to me. I often got home so late at night I didn't undress to sleep—just curled up in front of the fire in winter and out on the porch in summer. I was supposed to be at their house at five in the morning, no matter what the weather.

"It was decided that I would move in with the Jones family. I fixed myself a room in the shed off the kitchen. I had a cot with a fresh frizzled shuck mattress, sheets made from fertilizer sacks, and a pretty colorful quilt for a spread. There were old blankets from World War I stacked in a corner for cold days ahead. There was a lamp hanging on a nail with a metal reflector behind the globe, a white enamel pan to wash my feet in, towels made from sacks, and two sets of new work clothes. Best of all, I had three books on an upended box beside my bed: *Tom Brown's School Days, Aesop's Fables,* and another which I cannot remember.

"Under my cot I had a box with a lid that fastened. The box held my childhood collection: a few marbles, a jew's-harp, a rab-bit's foot, a penny, pieces of colored glass, a cooter shell, and my daddy's suspenders. The suspenders were the only thing left of my papa; the few clothes he had when he died were used to make clothes for the little ones. The suspenders were too long for me, so I made do with a piece of rope to hold up my pants.

"When winter came that year, it was decided that I would sleep in the room with Mr. Jones to keep the fire going and wait on him. Mrs. Jones was sick herself—she was able to keep hot food on the table, but no more jars of cookies and stack cakes.

"Winter evenings were long. Both Mr. and Mrs. Jones wanted to teach me to figure and learn something about the world outside the place where we lived. At one time they had been country school teachers, and they had books I was taught from. They both said they were sure I could pass the eighth grade examination; then if a school would hire me, I could teach. I did take the examination and did pass!

"Letters were written to kin in another state. They came and moved the old folks to a town about fifty miles away. When the day came for their moving, I was given sixty-one dollars for the time I had worked for my friends. They told me I would someday have a good job and be an asset to my state.

"Sixty-one dollars plus a cow and calf bonus was about the best news I could take home to Mama. This money was a fortune, not to be spent unless there was an emergency. We buried it under the chimney in a tin Blood Hound tobacco box.

"That summer I cut and hauled firewood for neighbors. Two dollars per cord was a good price. I was making enough to buy clothes to wear to high school. My heart was set on going, even though the school was ten miles away, and no transportation was furnished. I would have to walk or catch a ride.

"Shoes were the biggest drain on my money. The cost was three dollars for a pair of cowhide brogans, which were not very pretty, but they would stand the two-way walk each school day.

"In good weather I would start out barefoot to school; well before daylight I would be pounding the dirt road at a steady lope. My shoes would be carried in my striped hunting sack. On top of the shoes would be the lunch Mama had made the night before—a baked sweet potato and sugar-butter biscuit. Often when I reached school I would be so hungry that I would eat the biscuit and drink plenty of water. Then I would put on my shoes before going to class. Many other boys did the same thing, so anxious were they to get a good education.

"Those were hard years. At home two broken legs meant that we had to dig up the sixty-one dollars—each leg cost three dollars to set. Then Mama began to have toothache. One of her back jawteeth would pain her so bad that she would have to lie in bed with a hot salt bag on her jaw. After she had been in constant pain for several weeks, we went into the money again to hire someone to take Mama to the dentist; he discovered that the roots of the tooth had grown around the jawbone and were filled with holes. An operation of sorts was done. The trip and operation took twenty dollars of the saved money.

"Mama and I tried to save every way we could. Times were so hard there was no cash to pay day help. Mama gladly took produce for her work. Molasses was selling for twenty cents per gallon, eggs ten cents per dozen. There was no sale for garden vegetables.

"We lived on sweet and Irish potatoes, hog meat, molasses, collards, onions, turnips, cabbage, and cornbread. There were no biscuits at all, since a sack of flour cost seventy-five cents. When my cow came in fresh, how we rejoiced! Buttermilk, clabber cheese, cream on Sunday morning, and butter to spread on our cornbread when we needed a dessert. Mama would open a jar of plum preserves to go with the buttered bread. We had peanuts and hickory nuts for treats. Mama said she felt sorry for the squirrels when we scoured the woods for hickory nuts. We had some wild game, which we either caught in traps or killed by throwing green sticks at the squirrels or rabbits. There wasn't a nickle to spend on shells for Daddy's old gun. Here in my old age I am still a good stick thrower.

"The year I was in the tenth grade, our mule died, and the rest of the saved money went to buy another one. When we paid for the mule, I told the seller how I needed a few dollars to keep on hand for unexpected things, and he gave me back ten dollars, saying I could pay him when things got better.

"A neighbor asked me to help him kill and dress a beef. He paid me in meat, which was just what I wanted for Mama and the children: two big steaks, liver, the brains and kidneys, and all the fat from the insides of the steer. That night we had biscuits, gravy, and all the beef we wanted; that was the 'happiest-fullest' time we had seen in several years.

"Back then, there were only eleven grades at our high school. The head teacher said we were going to have a graduation exercise. I had the highest grades and would make the main speech. Parents were invited, and it was hoped they would make an effort to come. Mama was so pleased but was sorry too—she couldn't go, for there was nothing for her to wear. Since Papa died there had been no money for a new dress; she had only old clothes for her day work. She didn't want to shame me by wearing the only halfway fitting dress she had, which had been given to her by a sister years ago.

"I had a dollar or two left over from the ten the man let me keep when we bought our new mule. I was determined to buy dress material so Mama could make a dress to wear. At school the next day, I asked permission to go to the little crossroads town near our school where there was a store with a few bolts of cloth in the front window. I told the teacher my reason for going. She said her sister worked for the owner of the store, and that his wife was kind and helpful and would assist me in selecting material. I found cloth in many colors, some with vines and lots of blooms printed over the whole width of the bolt. There were so many colors I didn't dare make a selection.

"That night when I told Mama I wanted to buy material to make her a dress to wear to my graduation, she began to cry. She did not cry because she had done without—others were in the same fix and many people were hungry—but because, she said, she had grieved all these years because she had never been able to pay respects to papa and wear a proper dress to mourn him.

"Mama went to another store and bought cloth to make her dress and a simple hat to match. Perhaps some of the twenty-five people at the graduation wondered why Mama wore a solid black dress and a black hat turned up on one side decorated with a white rose. (The rose was snipped from a bush growing in one corner by the dirt chimney; the bush had been planted by my daddy the year I was born.) I knew and she did too that she was paying my papa the highest honor ever—that of wearing a mourning dress for him years after his death.

"I still have a picture of my mama. A man with a camera came to the graduation to make pictures of the graduating class and of anyone who had fifteen cents for a postcard snapshot.

"When Mama and I started the long walk home, I had my diploma tucked under one arm, my shoes in one hand, and Mama's hand in my other.

"We didn't have a dime in the world, not one cent to our names, but our hearts were calm and at peace. Mama had mourned Papa in a proper way. And we were looking forward to my class picture and the postcard picture of Mama that would be mailed to us soon, so said the photographer.

"That summer I got a job at a ground-hog sawmill for fifty cents a day, with dinner thrown in as part pay. Looking back, I realize the job was a hard one, tough and nasty. I stood in a pit under the mill where sawdust from the whirling blade fell. It was my job to shovel the sawdust out, throwing it up and out over my head.

"The other children at home had little outside farm jobs and brought their nickles and dimes home to Mama. Two of my little sisters, nine and ten, had the best jobs of all. Each morning they went along a woods path to the home of a family with two sets of twins, only a year apart. This family had fenced in a side yard with split rails, making a great place to play. The mother was sickly and expecting another baby before the summer was over. She sewed my sisters pretty dresses from material stored in a big trunk, gave them two good meals a day, and often sent extra food to us when her husband didn't get home by dark. My sisters said the husband wouldn't touch anything left over—his food must be hot off the stove.

"Times got better, and our family began to have a few of the necessary things in life. Not one of Mama's children had a run-in with the law; all got some education, and most bought small farms and built homes where they reared their children to be good solid citizens. I worked my way through college and taught school for many years. It was my pleasure to have students who went out into the world and made names for themselves and their state.

"Nothing has pleased me more than Mama coming to see me graduate from the eleventh grade, the first one to do so in either family." 🀰

Which Cat
Won the Fight?

Mama Cat watched over her nest of babies in the shuck pen at the big barn, hoping to keep the old tom cat from killing them.

Old Tom swished his tail in the cold moonlight, making little dust plumes in the bare side yard which the old woman had carefully raked and patterned in interesting designs with a brush broom. She was an artist by natural bent, not from training in school, and could copy anything in the dirt using sticks or brush broom. The past week the old woman had outdone herself making "Washington Crossing the Delaware."

Old Tom had completely beheaded Washington when he again started for the big barn. He wasn't the only cat to hear the silently calling voices from the dark—voices that only cats, not humans, hear. Along in the underbrush beneath the now-bare huckleberry bushes and knobby sweet gum sprouts crept Brindle, who lived in the woods by his wits and keen hearing. While other forest cats starved, it was Brindle who laughed in silent glee as irate farmers kicked house and barn cats and cuffed their dogs for eating half-grown barnyard chickens. They were innocent; Brindle was the guilty one.

Brindle and Old Tom heard the soft insistent voices in the chill December air—voices that seemed to say, "Come, come see what is waiting for you in the shuck pen at the big barn," and crept along at their own pace. Brindle bounded to a pine stump, sniffing the air, and was scared half out of his wits by a big owl who had mistaken him for an overgrown rat or rabbit. A stinging slash across his back drew blood and rankled his heart. Not being able to fight the now soaring owl, he felt the rage creep into his whole being. Something would have to pay for this.

Not stopping to lick his wound, Brindle bounded through the underbrush, forgetting to go on silent feet. Coming to the dirt road, he jumped from the clay bank at the highest point, making a loud plop as his belly raised a dust puff. Smelling his foe, he laid back his ears and began to creep forward—silent, relentless, angry—a seething mass aching for a snarling tumbling fight. Old Tom continued on his way seeking the baby kittens. His dim eyes were no good in the moonlight but his sense of smell told him danger was near. Thus two sworn enemies met, both on their way to answer a savage call in their black hearts to kill the baby kittens, four males and one female.

Once they had made their sudden rushes at each other, the kittens were forgotten and old scores were remembered: they were two males bent on destroying each other. Almost a match, they were half brothers and together had killed their father over a year ago after he had bested them for the favors of a town female cat that had come to live in the swamp near the old beech tree stand. Old Tom was a little soft with a spell of easy living since he had given in to seeking food at one of the tenant houses. His heart was strong, however, even if he was older than his brother. Brindle was a woods cat, used to battling other woods cats. In the past they had battled half the night, stopping only when the sun peeked through the pine forest toward the old dummy line and made the world an unsafe place to snarl and claw. Now the time was ripe, and one must die in the fight to the bitter end!

The battle raged up and down the roadbed, blood splotched the deep sand in ditches, and fur floated on the still night air, coming to rest on weed skeletons and making them bloom in December with unnatural flowers of black and brindle. In trees and bushes birds huddled and fluffed their feathers as if to shut out the fearful racket of death visiting two snarling, clawing, spitting and yowling cats. On and on toward the footpath leading across the west pasture the two cats battled, both growing weaker from loss of blood and from deep wounds to their self-importance.

Brindle lay down in the soft, scuffed, battle-roughed dust and, licking his paws, discovered two claws missing from one of them. Gently using the other, he touched a stump where only an hour or so ago a perfect ear grew; with his tongue he explored a long gash in his left hind leg. No matter that his right eye socket was dripping blood and the eye itself swung in gentle sway below his shredded lips—his heart was bursting with new energy and pride. At last he was ruler of Catdom.

Stalking as best he could past the limp mass of black fur that was the remains of Black Tom, he gave only a sniff: he was planning a smaller kill tomorrow night when he would take a sortie to the barn where five baby kittens waited. Mama Cat heard the fighting, and then the lull, which let her know one of the fighters had died. One more night her babies were safe. Her heart was tired, and weary was her body. The kittens were hungry and nursed often, pumping their tiny paws to make their mother let down her milk. She had not left their side for two days to hunt food, and the farm owners who brought food for her eating pan had no idea the house dogs came to gobble the warm milk and bread left each night.

One more night. Tomorrow night the winner would come to answer the silent call of the forest. The mama cat would fight, snarl, and claw, knowing full well that Brindle would overcome her puny efforts. This had happened three times before. Brindle was her son, born when she was a young cat, and he was the only one to survive the old woods tom who came to kill in the dead of the night.

Deep in her heart she knew her kittens were born to die. ▓

Jed, Sukie,
and Lin Yan

This is the story of Jed and Sukie, who lived in the backwoods of Amite County, and of the child, unwanted even by his mother, who brought radiant joy to their home.

Love is a funny thing; I know Jed loved his wife, Sukie, and she in turn loved him. These two were drawn together by a common bond that caused them to be unwelcome in homes in the neighborhoods about. They were not welcome in the homes of white people, nor were they at ease in the homes of black people, for they were of both blood.

Jed's love for Sukie was manifested in countless ways. The corn-cob box was always full of dry cobs for starting quick fires. The splinter box was never half empty in the years I passed their home with my father on our way to feed range cattle roaming fields in winter months. Stove wood was racked in tidy pigpens about the clean-swept back yard. Broomstraw, hanging golden red in the barn loft, was ready to use in brooms that would keep the three-room house neat and tidy. Jed saw to keeping the straw on hand year-round.

Jed scrubbed the brass-bound cedar bucket each Saturday, as he did the gourd dippers, keeping both fresh and clean, using nothing but white creek sand. Their front yard was swept once a week with dogwood limbs bound with bailing wire. Flower beds ornamenting the edges provided a safe place where favorite guinea hens could hide from a wandering fox anxious for a meal of tasty eggs or little babies just hatched. The front walk was sided with bottles in blue and brown. In full summertime, cockscomb and periwinkle plants grew in beds across the front of the house, blending with the rich colors of the bottles by the walk as well as the ones on the bottle tree just outside the front gate.

The two were married for many years, and each one lived for the other. When no children came to bless their home, Jed and Sukie asked some people they knew living in a town about 100 miles from Amite County to see if they could find a child who could be adopted. One day the mailman brought a letter from the distant town saying there was a child there who had been left behind by his mother when she decided to follow the primrose path to greener fields in

Chicago. The old grandmother had died and the child was being neglected, as there was no place for him.

A car was hired. Jed and Sukie made the long trip and brought home a little boy about four years of age, who had been so undernourished he could have passed for two years. Most of his life had been spent in a wooden box, so his legs hadn't developed enough for him to stand for more than a few minutes at a time. He was a little fellow with slanted eyes, black curly hair, and skin showing that his mother's people in distant years had lived in Africa.

The child had no clothes, not even enough to bring him home in. A blanket was bought to wrap him in until they reached Liberty, where hoarded egg money was used to pay for the hired car and driver. The rest of the money went to buy material to make soft shirts, trim pants, and sleepers for a child who had never had anything except a few rags thrown his way.

People wondered why Jed and Sukie took on such a burden—a child who could not walk, could not speak over ten words, and who uttered cries when anyone came close to his little bed. Those wondering didn't know the wealth of love, understanding, and happiness that dwelt in the hearts of these two, long shut away from the mainstream of life. Now the love that had been poured out on an orphan calf, a half-grown squirrel, a rabbit taken from the dogs before it was killed, mama cats and too many kittens—now this love went to the child.

A year passed. The child continued to grow strong and began to walk about the house holding onto the chairs, beds, and tables. He learned to talk and often chattered after the lamp was out at night. He sang to himself and was partial to the words, "Jesus loves me this I know, for the Bible tells me so." He had no idea what the words meant, but the tune comforted him.

The second year saw the child walking over the fields with his father to hunt rabbits for stews and soups. He was a shy child who often peered at the mail rider from behind his mother's skirts. He often asked to go beyond the end of the road where the big bend turned toward a creek where other children gathered to swim and swing from thick vines hanging from leaning trees over the swim hole.

After a sortie into the community neighborhood with a mess of fresh meat to a neighbor with many children, Sukie and Jed realized their child would be expected to go to school someday in the future. In their hearts they dreaded that day and decided to postpone it for a while.

A few years passed and the child was strong and healthy. He talked as well as Jed and Sukie. He knew the many ways country children entertained themselves: making corncob pipes, acorn cups and saucers, slingshots for hunting hawks, bows and arrows to shoot at bales of hay, and popguns for green chinaberries in season, setting hooks in the best places for fat mudcats and big fish in season. He could set snares to catch Mr. Fox and make bird traps to catch small birds to train and play with. He had a way with mockingbirds and kept several about the house that were free to come and go. They seemed to know the love in the home, and so they stayed and nested, raising young on limbs of trees that spread cooling shade over the cabin.

Finally it was decided that the child must get some learning. Sukie knew nothing about how to teach; in fact, she could not read at all. School was well over two miles from the child's home. To say he loved it would be wrong; however, he endured the taunts of the other children. Many was the time he came home with his clothes torn, telling his mother he had fallen down, when the truth was that the bigger boys had waylaid him, giving him a thrashing on general principles such as: since he had slanted eyes, was he Chink or Jap?

His clothes were cleaner than the other children's. His lunches were wrapped in a clean white cloth, and there were always good things to eat: fruit from town, sausage biscuits, jam tarts, and cracked nuts to share with the teacher—there was even a bottle of milk to put in the spring to keep cool until the noon recess.

Finally during the third year going to school became so unbearable for the child that Jed and Sukie decided to let him be happy at home.

How the days flew until he was eighteen. The young man tended a cotton patch and raised peanuts and other garden truck to sell in the small town. He bargained for and got a fast-stepping horse. Then his joy knew no bounds; the roads were his on summer evenings, as he rode to the Berwick Road and back around by Hog Eye Branch.

Peace and joy came to Jed and Sukie as they lived for and enjoyed having a son in the home. No more did Jed quit his plowing on hot summer days to come to the house to draw cool water for Sukie and the chickens. Now the son would bound from the fields with the strong sure steps of the young, draw water for his mother, grab a baked potato, and back to the fields he would go to put in a few more hours, until the sound of a stick beating on the side of the house would sound across the fields—time for a good dinner and being with his father and mother.

Suddenly this peace and happiness came to a swift close. One day when the earth was singing a song of wonder and beauty to all who would see, a strange car came to the clearing where Jed, Sukie and their son lived. A man in city clothes stepped from the car, took a paper from his pocket, and asked for Lin Yan Lee Jackson. It seemed as if the draft board had heard of a young man living in the backwoods who had never registered for the service.

And so it was that the young man left the place he had called home for fourteen years and went into the armed forces of the United States of America. A mere eighteen years of age, he was still a child in many ways, cunning in the ways of the woods, stalking unseen game.

In less than ten months he was on an island thousands of miles away from home; there he gave his life that others might live. It was a year to the day he had left home when the mailman brought a letter saying "killed in action." Life came to a standstill for Jed and Sukie. No longer did they have the homecoming of their child to look forward to.

Today the catfish swim in the creek, cows eat the fine green grass on the hillside, mockingbirds nest and sing in the trees around the homeplace. Sukie cooks her good custards and flat gingerbread cakes, often saving a portion for the child, forgetting that he will never return.

At night when Jed reads the Bible, the place is marked with the folded tasseled flag given them in honor of the death of their son. It is a very small flag to be sure, but it really doesn't matter, for the picture of a small child with slanted eyes is engraved on their hearts, and they often speak of the love they shared from the first moment they saw him sitting in the wooden box when he was four years of age. 🎎

Folks and Tales

A Teacher Who
Knew How to Teach

S he came to our one-room, curtain-across-the-middle school from another state, arriving in mid-September with her pretty clothes and a framed diploma. The diploma was decorated with pink and gold flowers and was signed with such a flourish, all scrolled and back-hand decorated, that nobody could read the name of the school or the signature on lines too short for the flowing loops and curls.

The letters attesting to her character and her teaching ability were stuck behind the clock in our front room (Daddy was head of the trustees and of course kept up with all mail in connection with the school). The letter had been read and passed around to the other trustees, who agreed that this teacher was just what the school needed.

Teacher was in her early thirties, and the board certainly hoped she wouldn't be sparking with the older boys. The last teacher had up and married her oldest pupil—went right off to Port Arthur, Texas, to live, without so much as saying "boo" to the five trustees. However, they couldn't say too much when four of them were related: the runaway teacher was daughter to one, daughter-in-law to another, granddaughter to the third, and niece to another, leaving Daddy the only non-relative.

Her relatives excused her on the grounds that "she was young and too smart. Why, she finished the eleventh grade when she was only sixteen and passed the teaching exam the following fall. Everybody knew Grady had had his eye on her for years—fact was, it was time he quit school and got a job and got married. He must be all of eighteen and still in the eighth grade."

It must be noted that even though the runaway teacher didn't say "boo" to the school board, neither did she give them the satisfaction of refusing to pay her last month's salary, all thirty dollars of it. As her mama said, "With a husband making right at sixty dollars a month running a streetcar, she wouldn't need to beg for pay that rightly should be hers."

The teacher who came to our school with an unreadable diploma was an excellent teacher. She taught children to read who had been in school for four years and were still looking at pictures in the Baby Ray reader. She made history come alive—as she talked, she drew chalk pictures on the blackboard. Long before up-to-the-minute educators were dreaming of flash cards, we at Enterprise school were learning our times tables this way. Teacher made everybody keep their hands on top of their desks when arithmetic class was being held. There was to be no counting on fingers—you either learned to do sums in your head or you stayed after school for an extra session.

It was this teacher who insisted that every tooth be brushed each and every morning before we came to school; as pre-Christmas presents, we got toothbrushes and tiny samples of toothpaste.

Teacher boarded at our house and was a constant source of pleasure and joy to our family. She praised Mama's cooking, expected the children to be mannerly, and advised Daddy to have his teeth pulled when they gave him misery. Daddy fattened up so much after getting store-bought teeth we began calling teacher "Miss Doc."

During recess, Teacher played games with us and seemed to get more pleasure than we did from playing games such as jump rope, hopscotch, farmer-in-the-dell, and tug of war. We made pinestraw play houses and would even make doll clothes on rainy days when we couldn't go outside to play.

Teacher sucked sweet nectar drops from honeysuckle blooms, nibbled and ate sheep sorrels when we did. We searched for shiny green sweet gum galls to suck, and she was pleased to make small May baskets using maypops from the passion flower vines. Our food scraps from noon school lunches were placed on a shelf just outside a side door. How we enjoyed seeing birds come to help themselves. We learned the names for the most common ones, looking up their proper names in a bird book which had belonged to Teacher's father.

We knew Teacher's parents had died the year before she came to teach at our school. She said she wanted to get away from scenes that reminded her of suffering and illness.

Teacher was born when her mother was well past forty and her father near sixty-five; she was a sickly child not able to attend school five miles away. Taught at home by her well-educated father, she knew more when her father presented her with the above-mentioned diploma than most college students did. At age fifteen she had passed all high school work. Then came eighteen years of tending ailing parents, and she studied college material when spare time was hers.

After she confessed she had never been to a real school, she wasn't re-elected at Enterprise. Teacher went to a church college, put her case before their board, was given many examinations, and in one semester went from being pre-primer to being a college graduate. In fact we learned many years later that she was a straight-A student.

Imagine how Teacher felt when she was told, "We hate to do this; however, you understand that we must have someone with at least an eleventh grade education and a real diploma to prove it."

We got a dilly of a teacher the next year—a man who had finished the eleventh grade. It took him fifteen years to get his diploma. He was given to bragging, "I never missed a day of school in all those years." 🈳

Mirrors

I like to remember Miss Sallie Primm and her husband Albert. An odd-looking couple, they were well past middle age the first time I saw them. He was well over six feet tall and very dark, with a white beard and a bald head. She was a dumpling, less than five feet tall, and wore her hair in fancy hairdos that took much curling, back-combing, and keeping out of damp weather. They dressed in wrapped-around clothes made from sacks.

They came to Grandmother Budd's back porch to ask if perchance she had a large piece of broken window glass she would swap for a setting of fuzzy-legged-bantam eggs, even-steven. Seems as if Miss Sallie had never had a looking glass. She had always kept her hair well-dressed by looking into the water-filled barrel under the house eaves. Due to the droughty conditions that summer, the barrel water was very low.

All who knew Miss Sallie and her neck condition felt compassion, since she could not bend her head more than a skimpy bit. Mr. Albert had dreamed up the idea of smoking one side of a flat piece of glass. He recalled his mama doing that very thing when her prized horn-backed mirror was stolen by bad boys who plundered and robbed in the lower community. The couple was pleased with the nice piece of glass they proudly toted home in a sack of moss and cottonseed.

Brother and I began asking to be taken to the little house behind the upper place. There was no road, only a winding footpath. We crossed the branch by walking on a fallen tree, which had had its limbs trimmed to make handholds.

We thought this outing such fun. We took buttered biscuits with pear preserves and patty sausage. The teacakes were so crisp they shattered at the first bite. Grandmother said we could drink from the ever-flowing spring at the mossy ledge near the hollow before the Primm house.

We were made welcome and took seats on sections of sawed logs on the shady front porch. Vines hanging with purple blooms, which in time would turn to velvet beans, ran rank everywhere you looked—over the top of the house and down the chimney into the fireplace.

Hens wandering on the porch looked at us with unblinking eyes, skirted our feet, and went into the front room where three of them hopped onto the bed and settled down to lay. One fussy hen parted the thick hanging vines in the fireplace and huddled over the hatching eggs. Several biddies peeked at us from under their mother's wings.

Brother and I wanted to see the mirror in the rain barrel, where Mrs. Primm had always looked to keep her hair well-dressed. Since we could lean over the barrel, we stood on a huge sandrock hoping to see our reflections in this unusual mirror. The water was so filled with wiggle-tails working, there was never a still surface to reflect our faces.

My grandmother asked Mr. Primm why he didn't empty the barrel. Didn't he know wiggle-tails hatched into mosquitoes, which were eating us alive as we sat on their porch?

He replied, "Now fancy that, reckon I won't. If the house caught fire we would need that water real bad."

We did get to see the mirror he had made for his wife by smoking the piece of windowpane he borrowed from Grandmother. It worked real well! 🎴

Glorious Dinners

The aged man took his seat, leaned back and said, "Rose Budd, I want to tell you about a time when I was a yearling boy living in Jefferson County with my parents, who were poor tenant farmers.

"We had the usual collards, turnip greens, Irish and sweet potatoes, some hog meat, molasses, berries and other wild fruit we were able to gather and can in season.

"The truth was we didn't know about good food many folks had on their tables. My father never had enough money to buy a hunk of cheese when he went to the commissary to buy meal, meat, flour and lard. You see, back then tenants living on a big farm had to get their 'rations' from the store on the farm. We were able to get credit and pay up when crops were gathered and sold.

"The man who ran the farm (for his brother who lived in another state) had no children. He often asked my father to let me work around his house, as his wife was sickly and could do no outside work. She was a good cook and stored the leftovers in a screened safe on the long back porch.

"How I enjoyed the days when the Mrs. had me put her horse to the buggy for a trip into town so she could visit the doctor and a lady friend. After she pinned on her wide-brim straw hat and pulled on driving gloves, she would put her hand on my shoulder and say, 'Now you and Barney have a good dinner. I have fixed a "Make-'em-eat-'em-up dinner."'

"How I delighted in those feeds! I hurried with my chores and joined Mr. Barney on the long back porch fixed up with chairs, a bench, the safe, and a table with places laid for two. If the mail rider had passed by I would get the mail, which often was nothing except the daily paper. Mr. Barney would read me the funny papers. He wanted me to stand beside him as he read the 'Gumps,' 'Katzen-jammer Kids,' 'Troonville Trolly Folks,' and others I have no remembrance about. I had never been to school at that time and was happy to have someone read to me.

"Often I would let my mind wander to the food in the safe and was glad when Mr. Barney told me to run to the back yard and ring the big bell so the field workers would know it was time to quit work and eat their dinners.

"After we washed our hands it was my job to put the food from the safe on the table—leftovers to be sure, but such goodies I had never seen! Cold chicken, dressing, a dish made of bits and dabs of fruit and dumplings, plenty of sweet thick juice and a crust over the top, nice and brown with slits cut so the juice had bubbled through and candied on top. Green beans with little Irish potatoes that had been drained and a vinegar dressing poured over. Cold biscuits, the tops slick with fresh butter and covered with lots of black pepper. Mr. Barney always urged me to take two at a time, saying his mama invented this way to use up cold biscuits.

"Before the blessing it was my pleasure to go to the smokehouse and get two bottles of root beer from a box filled with sawdust to help keep the block of ice from melting too fast. I felt fortunate to have this break from field work, often wishing I could swap places with my mother so she could have one of these dinners.

"There was a four-pound lard bucket washed and well aired sitting on the end of the table. This was for me to take any leftover dessert home to my sisters and brothers; always there was plenty to share. I often wondered if Mrs. made too much so that the children down the road could enjoy a treat. Looking back over the years, I know she did just that. When I got home in the afternoons, my sisters and brothers would be waiting for me. Each one would have a baking powder can lid and a spoon ready for the treat to be shared. They also wanted to hear everything I had done, especially about the dinner and the bottles of root beer. I can still recall my middle brother asking, 'Was it so cold it made your front teeth hurt?'

"Several years later the depression hit Jefferson County as it did the whole country. My father decided to pull up and go out to California. I didn't go with the family, but stayed on with Mr. Barney and his wife. She died the next year. The Texas brother lost the place to the Federal Land Bank, and Mr. Barney took to the roads looking for work.

"I joined the CCC camp and wound up in Alabama, married over there and later came to Mississippi to sharecrop. I never saw or heard from any of my family and didn't know how to go about looking for them.

"Of all of the things in my life, the dinners Mr. Barney's wife left for us stand out the most. Sometimes, Miss Rose Budd, I pray my middle brother had his share of root beer and it was cold enough to make his front teeth hurt." 🉐

Old Man
Sessums Carter

Old man Sessums Carter was sick, sicker than anybody realized. Hadn't he written for his children to come home? Yes, he wanted them around him in his last days. He was going to do real handsome by them. He was going to leave everything he had to his children, not to the church as he had often threatened when he shouted and yelled at his offspring, cursing the day they were born.

Oh, he was sick all right and had been "off" all his life if one could believe tales the neighbors told of the way he treated his family. Summer and winter everybody got up and went to the fields at the crack of dawn. He did let the wife and mother leave the fields at eleven to prepare the noon meal. When he was in a good humor, he would send one of the girls along to help her mother so they could get back to the field work by one sharp.

Certainly there was nothing wrong with hard work. All the families in the country were slaving to make a living, back in the days of five-cent cotton and ten-cents-per-dozen eggs (if you could find someone with a dime to buy them). The girls worked along with the boys: plowing, planting, harvesting, cutting wood, fixing fences, riving boards, building any shed or barn that was needed to shelter livestock or tools. The daughters went to the woods to hew crossties. They could take their place running the carriage at the ground-hog sawmill their father ran during off-seasons from the field work.

One hot summer day Mrs. Sessums died drawing a bucket of water. The bucket fell into the depths of the well, busting the well's sides and bottom wide open. Folks said Mr. Sessums raised more fuss over the well than the death of his wife.

Neighbors said a broken heart was the cause of Mrs. Sessums's death—a heart grieved that her daughters had no pleasures of the day, such as going to peanut boilings, possum hunts, bee tree robbings, and Sunday afternoon get-togethers held at the schoolhouse that served as a meeting place for both old and young in the community.

After the mother died, the boys and girls began leaving home to shift for themselves, taking jobs doing anything to earn a dollar. The girls were good plain cooks and could wash, starch, and iron as well as commercial laundries and much cheaper. Strong and healthy, they often worked around the clock when work was to be had. Habits of childhood were deeply ingrained, and they too saved every penny not needed to keep body and soul together; that is, until enough money was on hand to get a "course" in the line they chose to follow.

Two girls were beauty shop operators. Two opened a restaurant near the shipyards and made good livings serving country-style meals to those who wanted plenty of food and wanted it cooked "home style."

Two sons took mechanics courses and opened their own shops, turning out first-class work. One son joined the navy to see the world; he went to school and at one time worked on the projects helping to put a man on the moon. Another son found he had a flair for meeting people and could sell things to people to make their lives better. Insurance became his field after he tried his hand at various kinds of door-to-door selling. Years ago I saw his picture among the nation's million-dollar insurance club members.

Now these children were gathered from all parts of the nation at their father's request—men and women who had started from nothing but hard work and homegrown food plus cast-off clothing from relatives who, if the truth had been known, had less than old man Carter did (had saved and hoarded, that is).

Yes, old man Carter was a-feared he was going to die. Three months before, he had seen his brother buried; he had died a bad death from a cancer on his neck. Another brother was right at death's door with the same trouble—a mole on the back of his neck had suddenly gone wild. Before he was laid low, he suffered so much pain the modern painkillers gave him no ease. Hadn't the father of old man Carter died with the same kind of mole trouble? Every day the mole on the back of Mr. Carter's neck felt hot and burned. He took to turning his shirt collar inside so it wouldn't rub across the top of the mole. Now it felt puffed and full of fever. He had pains and often awakened in the night with a chill and the feeling that he was going to die.

The first day his children were at home, old man Carter handed out the will he had made himself, showing that he was leaving his children $84,000 in cash. He made a speech to the effect that he was happy to see them all doing so well. He couldn't understand why his daughters cried and wailed, "Why didn't you let us have pretty clothes and a living room set when we were girls?''

Over the next two days the money was gathered in one pile, and the greenbacks were divided among the children. They didn't linger long.

Old man Carter decided he better see a doctor about his neck. He felt so poor now that his money was gone (all except what was hidden in the barn), he decided to go to the new doctor in town. More than likely he didn't have many patients and would be willing to take a couple of dollars to give his opinion on the length of time Mr. Carter had to linger in this world of pain and ungrateful children. (By this time regret was setting in and a bitter brew was simmering over the gone-gosling money.)

The doctor was young, hardly dry behind the ears. He listened while old man Carter told of his father's and brother's deaths, and about how another brother was at death's door, all because of moles turned into cancer. Mr. Carter explained that a mole on his neck was about to kill him, that he had cancer in the worse form. He wanted assurance that he wouldn't be allowed to die a hard death. He also said that he had very little money now that he had given all of it away to greedy children.

Tenderly Mr. Carter unwrapped the soft white hankerchief from around his neck and bowed his head so the doctor could get a good look. Then he got the most awful shock of his life. The young doctor began laughing. He laughed so hard he finally excused himself to go catch his breath and get rid of the hiccups, leaving his patient to fume, cuss, and stomp his foot.

When the doctor returned, he explained to Mr. Carter that there was nothing wrong with the mole on his neck except that a tick had settled beside it, had turned to a dog tick, and was ready to burst and disgorge her brood. ▨

Mission of Mercy

D ay before yesterday I opened the old armoire in our smoke-house, took down a tin box wrapped in oilcloth, tucked the box and its contents into a striped ticking sack, along with a catch-as-catch-can sort of lunch, tied my straw hat on, and whistled to our house pet, Lady, a very proper Boston. We were going on a mission of mercy.

Down the big road we went, stopping to see interesting tracks in damp sand beside the winding trail we later took. We drank from a deep blue hole in Waggoner Creek where I admired my freckled face. We crept across a fallen beech tree, which spanned the best fishing place in Amite County, and flushed a covey of quail at the toe of the hill leading to the Gene House, where ghosts are said to romp and play nightly.

I was on my way to visit Maggie Sorendo, who lives alone—that is, if you do not count cats—if you do, she has plenty of company. There are six grown mother cats, three battle-scarred toms, and many half-grown kittens living under and on her back porch.

One thing I can say about the Sorendo cats is that they have lovely manners. They will twine about your legs, lick your offered finger (if greased) with gently rasping tongues, or pat your shoulder as you pass by a fence post with a paw full of nicely tucked-in claws. Never do they climb the kitchen screen door to beg for food when people are eating.

You see, my effort to do-unto-others for Maggie involved cutting her toenails. Maggie is quite fat and can't see her feet when she sits, much less lean over and get anywhere near her toes. Mother Nature handed Maggie a short deal in the arms department; her arms are no longer than those of a six-year-old child.

She trusts me, but it's an honor I'd give away if she would let someone else be in her favor. You see, the nail-cutting takes a whole day, with the going and coming, visiting and looking through various trunks and old boxes packed with things given to her over the past seventy years. The job itself is nerve-wracking. Thank goodness her nails grow slowly so they only need cutting twice a year. (I'd visit for fellowship more often.)

The box holds various snippers, clippers, and files given into my keeping just before Maggie's husband died. They are beautiful instruments made from finest steel. Where they came from Maggie doesn't have an idea. Maggie is so ticklish about her feet that getting near them is almost like putting your life in her hands. Even a gentle touch on the bottom of either foot will cause it to jerk and twitch, even kick out hard. Then she goes into bursts of laughter, shaking all over. She must breathe into a paper bag, the same air over and over; then she can stand the nail-cutting. We get the job done.

We sat on her front porch steps eating the lunch I brought: ham biscuits, pear tarts, and a slice of watermelon. We saved the melon seeds for her coop of bantam hens, little hens with feathered legs and top-knotted heads.

Maggie told me to look deep into a red trumpet vine near the front steps to see two hummingbird nests. I was cautioned not to breathe into the nest—if I did, the mothers would quit the nests. The nests were the size of thimbles, each with three very tiny eggs.

She wondered if I would be kind enough to go up the hill to see if her guinea hens had more than four eggs in each nest. She reminded me to go one way and come back another, as the guinea hens are always on the lookout for reasons to find other places to lay, and a tromped-down path to and from the nests would be reason enough. She handed me a scalded, long-handled wooden spoon to remove the eggs from the nests. She said to get the freshest looking eggs and leave four, since she is sure her hens can count. She cautioned me to hurry back if I wanted to look through an old steamer trunk we have never taken time to plunder.

The treat for my day's visit was a five-layer stacked cake with mayhaw jelly between the layers. The nicely browned layers were so thin the jelly was almost their equal. The cake was made rich yellow with guinea eggs, and baked in a wood stove that belonged to her mother in 1899, the year Maggie says she was born. How delicious the cake was with cold sweet milk for our late-night snack! 🥮

Miss Dillon's Hats

"There goes Miss Arie Dillon, rushing the season," so Mama would say when Miss Dillon showed up at gatherings wearing an out-of-season hat. Not that Miss Dillon was striving to be stylish or in the swim of fashion. Neither was she trying to keep up with the nowadays-popular Jones family—indeed not!

When Miss Dillon decided to go anywhere, she went as she was dressed. She simply removed her apron, fluffed the pompoms on her soft leather house slippers, rubbed a cold biscuit over the toes, peered at herself in the wavy front-room mirror, tucked up her scolding locks with two pompadour combs set with brilliant rhinestones, reached for a hat, turned the cuffs of her long-sleeved dress down over her hands, and away she went. (She believed that no well-bred lady appeared with head and hands uncovered.)

She was apt to show up wearing her long-gone-to-his-reward father's black derby, complete with a tarnished gold button extolling the virtues of William Jennings Bryan, "The Peerless Leader," who was candidate for president of the United States in 1896.

If the derby wasn't to hand she was likely to sashay into church wearing a "Charlotte Corday" hat, said to be all the rage back in 1905. I remember the hat. Each time I saw Miss Dillon wearing it, I thought, "Whoever dreamed up that awful thing certainly didn't like women."

Imagine my delight when I came across a description of the Charlotte Corday hat in the book *The Good Old Days* by David Cohn. He copied directly from the 1905 Sears, Roebuck "wish book": "The very latest hat is known as the 'Charlotte Corday.' At present, it is the rage of Paris and New York. A small dress shape with edge drooping in mushroom effects. The large bell crown is developed in gathered and shirred brown silk. On the left is a wheel rosette, and six large brown silk-and-velvet flowers elegantly arranged in front on the large bell crown complete the trimmings of this hat."

In 1925 if Miss Dillon had been trying to keep up with other women as to style, according to a fashion magazine she would have worn a hat of satin. The article said: "Most heartily do we urge every woman who desires to keep in style to wear a hat of satin. Fashion has been generous with satin; it is not confined to a short season in spring, summer, fall or winter. Satin hats are seen during all months in the smart style centers."

My mother, along with her women friends and relatives, did their best to keep in fashion, not rushing the season nor lagging too far behind.

Miss Dillon continued to amaze folks with an array of bonnets, woolen caps, even a miner's cap complete with carbide light that belonged to a distant relative who went to the coal fields somewhere in the East. Her favorite was her papa's derby.

Alas, William Jennings Bryan did not become president of the United States, though he was runner-up to William McKinley, who was a Methodist and a lawyer. McKinley was the third president to be assassinated in office. 🀙

Aunt Lue's
Thrifty Ways

This summer I creamed corn from green cobs, which in turn were saved for feeding the cow at milking time. Chopped into small pieces and mixed with tender shucks and a handful of cottonseed meal, the cob shuck salad was special for the cow and her calf, which was just beginning to nuzzle in the feed box.

Cobs have played many roles on Shady Rest; they have been used for everything from making quick fires to providing games for children. Cobs were used to make doll babies and to outline rooms on the ground when we played house under the trees in summer. We made great piles of them for beds and chairs (we never tried to sit on them; they were just for looks).

When corn for the grist mill was shelled at the barn, the person doing the shelling was careful to take the cobs home to store for a time when firewood for the stove was scarce.

Aunt Lue lived beyond our house in a small three-room cottage sheltered by a tall, spreading chinaberry tree.

After cutting fresh green corn from the cobs, Aunt Lue would boil the cobs in water to cover. The resulting liquor was made tasty with butter, lots of black pepper, a pinch of sage, and a smidgen of salt. The result was a delicious corncob soup, which was served in a teacup and sipped with care. The soup would be blazing hot from her dried corncob fire.

If there were few berries or fruits for jams, jellies or butters, Aunt Lue would boil red corncobs, strain off the liquor, add apple juice canned the fall before, sweeten with honey, and boil it down until it "sheeted" from a spoon. She would store this reddish-pink jelly in stone crocks so that she and her grandson Hezzi Ki could enjoy spreading it on hot buttered cornbread.

Aunt Lue made sure she got her share of cobs from the house barn. The third room of her house had a corner where piles of cobs were kept for starting fires in her tiny wood stove and fireplace. In another corner were a few turns of stove wood. The third corner was reserved for her prized box plants once cold weather came. The fourth corner held Hezzi Ki's single cot. To make sure dry fireplace wood was always on hand, he kept two armloads of small sticks under the cot. Summer and winter, there was a big green stick of wood at the back of the fireplace. Never allowed to blaze, it was there to throw out heat.

If Aunt Lue wanted to heat her coffee "real smart" (which meant fast), she would rake a few coals to the hearth, pile on chipped cobs, and place her blue granite coffee pot in the middle of the smouldering cobs.

When we visited, she made water bread for us this way: she would make a quick cob fire under the first stove lid, get the kettle boiling, pour hot water over sifted cornmeal, add a dab of hog lard, and mix by hand. Very thin pones were patted out by hand and baked on the pitted stove lid. Some were worn through, causing the water bread to have a delightful smoky taste. We never had butter on these bits of bread, only syrup. How delicious it was if the syrup was low in the can and there was soft sugar to be dipped and spread on the cakes, often stacked three high.

Aunt Lue had butter on hand for her regular customers. She never wasted one drop of milk. She drank one cup warm and fresh from the cow and strained the rest in stone crocks. This was allowed to sour, and the skimmed cream was churned to butter for those who wanted pints of butter made this way. Two pounds of butter would be put in a heavy boiler over a slow cob fire. It was a laborious job to render down this butter to make two pints that were pure grease. Rendered butter could be sealed and kept for at least a year, if it was stored in the darkest corner of a pantry. For this amount of butter Aunt Lue was paid fifty cents. Time wasn't worth much, and her cow grazed up and down the countryside or wandered in my father's pastures with his cows.

Aunt Lue could buy many things with fifty cents: a bar of sweet (bathing) soap, spool of thread, one pound of sugar, coal oil, a clay pipe bowl, Blood Hound chewing tobacco, and green coffee beans. Each of these items cost five cents. She was very thrifty: she parched the green coffee beans, used a short section of creek bank cane for stem to her pipe, chipped the chewing tobacco very fine and packed it tight in her pipe. The sweet soap was used only for first Sunday church bathing; lye soap was used at other times.

The leftover fifteen cents would be saved until enough was on hand to buy six yards of material for two quilts and four spools of quilting thread. The quilt tops were made from good parts of old clothing or saved scraps from new materials given Aunt Lue by a lady who sewed for the public. Cotton batting for the quilts was made from cotton picked in the fields after harvest and before cows were turned in to "eat out" the fields. Aunt Lue and Hezzi Ki spent their spare time picking seeds from locks of cotton. Then batts were made using a pair of cards.

In summer, quilting frames would be placed outside on straight-backed chairs, and women who wanted to visit would help out by putting in a few rows of quilting (all except Essie Plume who was left-handed and always made a mess of her own quilts). These nice heavy quilts were sold for two dollars. I am sure that if one of these colorful quilts could be found today, it would be considered a real piece of folk art and would bring several hundred dollars. ▨

A Hard Life

T he events in this story are true; only names have been changed to permit the main character to live in peace for the rest of her days. This is her story.

"'Course you don't recall me—you was a fat chubby little girl when I went to the pen. Must have been in 1923 when I took up living at that big old farm known as Scorch Plant.

"I fully agree 'twant nothing funny about working from 'can to can't' with the threat of the strop, "White Fanny," hanging over a-body's every move. No, I never had the strop laid cross my back but once, and that is the reason I wrote you to come see me.

"You want to know why I was sent to Scorch Plant? My papa made me marry old man Zebbert Hubbard—me only fifteen years old and him with not one tooth in his gums, bald as an egg, couldn't eat a thing but pap and such, expected me to live on the same when my body cried out for greens, fat meat, chicken, parched peanuts and quinces. Wouldn't let me chew sugar cane 'cause he couldn't.

"All the chickens I raised he sold to a passing peddler, then put the dimes and two-bit pieces away somewhere where I could never find them.

"I tell you for fair I just didn't like old Zeb and dreamed of the day he would turn up his toes and give up the ghost, so I would be free to marry a boy over in the next community who cut his eyes at me every first Sunday when he passed our house on his way to the Holiness Church up the hollow a piece. We'd be sitting on the porch in good weather, or I'd be drawing a bucket of water, rain or shine in the winter.

"Law, no, I never went anywhere, just worked from daylight to dark in Zeb's little piddling patches. When Zeb left the house for trips to the settlement store, he chained me to a wall in the pantry. In summer I almost smothered and froze in the winter. No, my pa wouldn't help me none, didn't believe in coming between man and wife. I always suspected Zeb paid Pa a few dollars to make me marry him.

"Hawks started taking my biddies one summer. I was almost seventeen that year, and even though I never got so much as a pretty hair ribbon from the sale of my fryers, I hated hawks swooping down and taking the biddies off.

"Zeb chained me up and made a trip to the railroad town where he bought a big box of Nux Vomica to be mixed with grease, which then was smeared on the heads of the chickens. When the hawks ate the heads, the Nux Vomica would kill them. If you didn't get enough on, the hawk just got sick and seemed to build up to the point where even a whole lot wouldn't kill him.

"Right about then I decided to start eating one grain of the stuff every day for a few days, then go to two grains, and so on until I could stand a real dose without it killing me. I had plans for Zeb.

"Things rocked on for a time. My body was built up to take a whopping dose of Nux Vomica without it bothering me.

"Zeb didn't fare too well the day we both ate the same amount. The fact was, his toes turned up and that was the end of Zeb. I thought that was that, but it wasn't. I was brought to trial and sent to the pen for forty-two years. Seems like I swapped one sort of life for more of the same, and I didn't have the boy from the next community to look forward to once a month.

"At the pen we wore shift dresses, long down to our ankles, and nothing else. We were hot in summer and suffered in cold winter. Word came to our camp in 1930 that underdrawers were going to be supplied to every female at the camp. It seemed that some good ladies yearned to uplift and help the women inmates and hit on the idea of unbleached domestic drawers as the very thing.

"The woman overseeing the sewing was left-handed, and every last pair of underwear opened on the wrong side. All were made the same size—not one pair in ten fit. We were forbidden to swap for a better fit.

"After a few days we had a sit-down after the boss lady refused to listen when we said we were not going to wear those unhandy drawers. It was scorching summer at that time! I tell you, when that strop "White Fanny" came into play, it was laid on with a heavy hand by a mean woman who wanted to toady to the boss lady so she could have sugar instead of molasses in her coffee.

"Sure, they made us wear them, whipped us into submission. However, those drawers began to disappear. No matter how hard the trustees searched, not a pair turned up; that is, until wintertime came and vegetables from the canning factory and the five-gallon cans of corn, peas, and beans were opened to prepare food in the kitchens. Every female in the pen worked in the canning plant and we had canned our drawers!

"Forty-two years is a long time to be gone from around here. I paid for my error to society. You want to come to my wedding next Saturday?

"Who am I going to marry? The same boy—I mean man, now—that used to cut his eyes at me on his way to the Holiness Church. His wife passed away ten years ago, and he wants me to do his cooking." 🀫

Greener Pastures

L ast week in the company of some fine conversationalists, the subject of "greener pastures" came up—pastures that belonged to someone else or that were outside the law. The company discussed pros and cons on many subjects relating to this green pasture theme.

One man said he knew a person who had embezzled from a loan company, served a short sentence, and apparently lived for several happy years on the money stolen. But—was he happy? Did his green pasture turn out to be the vitamin-packed grass he thought it would be or did bitter weeds grow tall?

One family I knew did much better because of greener pastures.

I remember Tempie's husband, Sam, who wandered far afield in the greener-than-green pastures making corn liquor (white lightning)—the illegal backwoods brew so desired years ago. (I hear whispered tales that today it can be made and sold for around twenty-five dollars a gallon, with no complaints about the quality.)

Tempie's husband made his liquor in the old dummy line draw. The tidy little still was in a hidden hollow. There were liderd knots for the hauling to cook the brew off, plenty of children to tote water from the wet weather branch, free glass jugs from a town drug store, and best of all, customers ready and waiting for the dew that dribbled from Sam's cooker a drip at a time. He did not bother to color his corn liquor with burned sugar but sold it clear as spring water; however, it was said that his dew was so high-proof he could cut it one-eighth with water.

Finally law and order, in the form of men from the big city up the railroad (namely Jackson, Mississippi), came snooping around. Daddy wasn't too pleased to see these men, but they were invited to eat dinner with us. They enjoyed Mama's mutton roast along with blackberry dumplings and other farm food.

Using big axes and their mighty muscles they "stove" in Sam's cooker, chopped the copper tubes into little pieces, and kicked the liderd pile down. To add insult to injury, they chunked rocks at the glass jugs waiting to be filled. In Tempie's words, "Sam's goose is cooked."

After a trial, Sam was sent to Parchman.

There was a crop in the fields which needed plowing by a grown man. Tempie and the children made out with help from her father and brothers who lived up Hog Eye Branch.

Being as there was no welfare back then, Tempie "took the bull by the horns" and borrowed a still from an old man in the hills across Waggoner Creek, who had grown so old he had to give up stilling. With the money from several batches of white lightning (she simply took over Sam's customers), Tempie bought fertilizer for next spring's farming and food to see them through the winter. She and the children farmed without the father and husband.

At the end of that fall there was money to stash in the shuck mattress. This went on for the time Sam was in the pen. The children had shoes; a new well bucket with rope was bought; window panes were added to the window frames and the wooden shutters were used for firewood.

Sam got out of the pen six months early for good behavior and because someone had put in a good word with the governor. When Sam came home, he found enough money in the mattress to make a small down payment on a few acres to call his own.

One thing he learned at the pen was to rise early and go to bed at dark. He also learned a few good farming tips, which he applied to his new farm. I recall one thing he was proud of about his stay in the pen—he was quick to tell that he had never had the strap called "Black Annie" laid across his back.

Sam and his family seemed to prosper from his sortie into green pastures of illegal liquor making. 🎴

A Gift
for Gardening

A unt Lue was a master gardener in her heyday—so said others who lived near or on my father's farm where she and her grandson Hezzie Ki lived. When I began to help in the gardens and yards, Aunt Lue was my teacher. She planted "by the signs," regardless of the weather. She had several gardens and always "hit" something just right.

Her first garden of the season was on the hillside near Agnes Branch. No matter if the rains were heavy and the earth a soggy mess in the bottom where most planted their spring gardens, Aunt Lue had her rows laid out so there would be good drainage. She gathered spring lettuce and green onions and pinched off tender leaves from last year's old collard plants. Nearby would be wild pokesalat plants with finger-high leaves begging to be made into the ever-popular "salat" country people depended on to clean their bloodstreams from winter ills thought to be lurking therein.

The first of April saw her big garden planted in the peaceful bottom beside Waggoner Creek, where gardens had been tilled since the first resident settled in a cave there. Her garden was easy to water in dry weather; no matter how low the creek became, there was the boxed-in spring nearby where water could be dipped to pour around each plant.

Fall gardens were always abundant. "Lazy families" was Aunt Lue's name for those who hoped to beg or borrow from her, or who didn't cultivate with whole heart but let weeds take over or wandering hogs and calves eat their garden sass. Not so Aunt Lue; these fall gardens were her way of making spending money for things needed and wanted to keep her household going.

Bunches of collards, turnips, and green onions went for five cents per bunch. The greens would fill a big black iron three-legged cookpot with good eating when served with hoecake and pot liquor. She had sweet potatoes in earth banks and fall onions drying in long strings with the tops plaited—two onions for a copper penny. Fall Irish potatoes were never dug unless they were being sold or were needed for home eating. Well into the winter months, "new" Irish potatoes could be had for cooking milk-gravy dishes or making wax-like potato salad. This delightful old lady had several crocks of salted-down or water-glassed eggs, one cent each.

Once the gardens of Aunt Lue were broken and harrowed by her grandson, she took over the working with her hoes. One was a very heavy hoe made from a piece of metal from the old watermill on Waggoner Creek. Dale has this hoe and also enjoys working with it. He wonders how the little old lady weighing around 100 pounds could hold out!

Her dearest farm implement was a dainty hoe, surely wider when new than when I first saw it. By then it was very narrow, no wider than the faded ribbon band around her Sunday-go-to-meeting hat. This narrow hoe was kept greased with pure lard, wrapped in a dried sheepskin against rust. Aunt Lue used it for special hoeing among dainty garden and flower plants. She never wasted a motion when getting grass removed—five passes with the hoe was all it took. This little hoe, a real treasure, is now mine!

We spent time running errands for her: fetching seeds to replant, or a coal from the fireplace to light her clay pipe, or a swallow of coffee from the beside-the-fireplace pot. We would bring her face rag to lay across her forehead under her bonnet (this kept sweat from running down her face), or go to the branch to get water to freshen her mouth.

Once she had finished her garden work, we were instructed to break leafy limbs from low-growing bushes and then to walk backwards, brushing away all signs of footsteps. Spirits, haints, ghosts, and other night things would not dare to venture into such a garden.

Often we were rewarded with fried bread. Cornmeal would be mixed with spring water and the batter patted out on top of an eye on the wood stove and fried to a crisp. We ate these little cakes with cream and syrup sugar from the bottom of the syrup can. ▧

Pa Jim

I am happy that our sons have had the pleasure of knowing Pa Jim; into every child's life should come such a person. He is one of the fortunate people who believes that life everlasting is just over the hill, and that it behooves each person to strive for goodness here on earth, the better to wear the heavenly golden crown already engraved with his name.

Pa Jim hasn't had much education from school books; he will tell you his education came from "The University of Hard Knocks." Left an orphan at age five, he went to live with a great-uncle who wandered the countryside preaching to trees and asking for handouts whenever he felt the need for food. Pa Jim tells of eating flatbread and drinking branch water, making do with berries and other fruit he could gather in the fields and woods.

When the children of Pa Jim and Ma Carrie left home for jobs in the North or in California, they left space in the five-room home as well as in the hearts of their parents. When grandchildren came along, often they were sent to the Collins grandparents. If there wasn't bed space to sleep the little fellows, Ma Carrie would make a pallet on the floor during the summer and snug five or six little ones into the same bed when winter winds howled around the chimney. Clothes for these grandchildren are made by Ma Carrie, who is quite deft at taking a sack and cutting a shift that will fit either boy or girl.

Six small children playing in a drift of white sand could be either boys or girls. Their hair grows in curls and soft polished ringlets; their liquid brown eyes are long-lashed and deeply set. Pat a child on the shoulder and say, "How are you, little girl?" and likely there will be a flash of white teeth, a low laugh and, "I'm not a girl! My name is Rob. I am Mary's middle child." Pat another and feel safe to call this one a boy, but it's a mistake again—she is Melody, the fifth child of Sarah, who lost her husband to an alligator down in Florida.

You give up and go to the barn where Ma Carrie is beating out velvet beans to feed her milk goats. She cautions you to stand up-wind, as the fuzz from the bean hulls travels far on the slightest breeze. She recalls the time a tramp slept in their barn in a pile of velvet beans; the next morning they saw him running and clawing himself on the way to the branch where he stayed the better part of two days trying to get eased from the stinging of the fuzz.

Pa Jim isn't afraid of field work, but he feels he does more good for the community when he goes about riding his one-eyed mule doctoring the sick and ailing animals of his friends and neighbors. True, he will doctor the sick animals of his sworn enemies (he has very few). However, the rate of their recovery is astonishingly low beside the recovery of animals belonging to his friends: one in ten for enemies, eight out of ten for friends.

Pa Jim says the ones that die have been "give up on" before he is called, or they belong to folks who have put a "conjer" on him, given him the back side of their bad talk. The time he had the "conjer" on him, he had to take time out and go far into the swamp bottom of Waggoner Creek to seek out herbs and other secret things to make a different, stronger "conjer" than had been put on him.

He takes his doctoring plunder in a large sack made from a water buffalo hide; where he got the hide is uncertain. Our oldest son insists that the hide is nothing more than an old bull hide turned wrong side out with the hair inside. (This talk is out of Pa Jim's hearing, mind you.) The sack is filled with wonderful herbs, salves, and tall bottles of vile-looking and still more awful-smelling waters.

This I do know: many a time when the town horse doctor has been to look at a sick animal, shaken his head, and said, "Well, I would call the deadman-wagon for this critter," my father has sent for Pa Jim.

He always comes at a quick trot, his old mule in a lather from pulling the long hill behind the Gene house. He makes all lookers-on stand back as he doctors with this and that, rubs and pats, leans over and whispers in the sick animal's ear. Most of the time his doings work; sometimes we have waited too long. This is a troubled time for Pa Jim. He feels a grieving weight on his heart and extracts promises from all that next time he will be sent for at the first sign of sickness among our animals.

If he has time, Pa Jim will treat our sons to the tales about Hard Times being a guest in most of the homes in Amite County. He will tell about the time Kyle Green's blind mule had the staggers and fell into a pile of glass windows for the new room. This was a room to replace the one taken off by a tornado just as smooth as a beaver slide, so easy that the table lamp in the next room wasn't bothered; in fact Kyle got his Bible and read scripture to his wife

Leathie, who was abed with a sick headache.

They love the story about Old Man Moses, who kept his mule in the bedroom where he and his wife, Mollie Annie, slept with their triplets and two sets of twins. When push came to shove about the mule in the bedroom, the mule didn't move out—the wife and children took up sleeping in the mule stall.

Lest you send for Pa Jim to doctor on your sick goat, please don't. Once he was bested by a goat; that story is told often loud and long. If Pa Jim is around he sneaks away, going home to sit among his grandchildren and lick his wounds, remembering the time a big billy goat got the best of him. However, this is a story for another time when fires burn low and winds blow around house eaves. 🐚

Leathie and Her
Bag of Special Spices

B ack in my young days when special company was coming, a note would go to the home of Kyle and Leathie Green saying, "Please come cook dinner for me on Friday. Be sure to bring your little bag."

Bright and early on the morning when company was expected, we would hear a steady bellowing at Waggoner Creek flat. We would leave our breakfast, rush down the road to the creek, and hitch a ride on the two-wheeled cart drawn by the two blind oxen that were trained by Kyle to pull him and Leathie over the countryside. (Of course everyone knows that when blind oxen smell or go over running water, they bellow.) The steady bellowing was our signal for a good little joggly ride.

Leathie would come into the kitchen beaming and shooing people out of her way. The aforementioned "little bag" was placed on the kitchen fireplace mantle and never mentioned by others. It held her secret herbs and spices. (When Leathie died the secret of her herb chicken dumplings went with her.)

Always she furnished her own aprons, snow white, the old-time wraparound kind. She also wore a winged white cap to match, low on her forehead, with "Bless This Food" stitched in black across the front. Leathie brought her own pot lifters, great padded ones which never let the heat through. Mama was always saying she was going to make some for our kitchen, but she went right on using folded rags and burning her hands when she lifted heavy skillets and black iron pots from this hole to that one on the great monster of a wood stove.

Milk-fed fryers had been dressed and salted well before daylight, and Irish potatoes had been boiled with eggs for Leathie to make her famous fried chicken and potato salad.

If it happened to be strawberry time, Brother and I would sit under the back yard pecan tree to hull berries, eating as we hulled, until Leathie stepped to the back porch to say, "I know what y'all are doing, eating the big ones—stop that right now, you know that's not fair." The two-quart bowl of big ones and a half-gallon of small ones went to the kitchen to be turned into the most delicious short-cake ever. Sweet cream in a quart glass jar would be let down in the well bucket to be chilled so it would whip just right at the last moment before the cake was served.

Dinner was special: snap beans cooked with side meat and seasoned with an herb that sharpened the bean taste, new Irish potatoes in milk gravy smooth as cream and speckled with snippets of green onion tops, chicken fried golden brown and butter tender inside, pan gravy to dip over big biscuits, flat and crisp on the bottom, rounded tall on top, garden lettuce wilted down with bacon grease and hard-boiled eggs, folded together with a pinch of the herbs and spices from the bag on the mantle.

Buttermilk was a must with this meal. The golden-layer strawberry shortcake was the crowning glory. Portions were served in regular soup plates, so the juice and whipped cream could meld and be enjoyed. Other food might be left, but never the shortcake—Leathie would have had her feelings hurt if this had happened.

Town folks tried to entice Leathie and Kyle to move to town. They promised good wages, electric lights, running water and picture shows. Leathie and Kyle knew they would never be happy away from their small farm. Leathie's heart was buried under tall pines near their modest home where nine little graves were. None of their babies had lived more than a month.

When Leathie died, Kyle tried to do his own cooking, or as he said, "I burn for myself." He lived near Pa Jim and Ma Carrie, who were good neighbors. One day Pa Jim invited Kyle over to live with his family, as he could see Kyle was losing too much weight trying to eat his own cooking. This didn't work out as Kyle liked to stay up most of the night blowing on his French harp and sleeping until nearly ten o'clock the next morning. ▨

Jimson Yarber

J imson Yarber's home is a tiny cabin nestled under an oak tree that has stood for a hundred years. Its two rooms—a living room and a room where basket-making supplies are stored—are all the home Jimson needs and wants.

Woods grow right to his door. Squirrels jump from the sheltering oaks to the roof of his cabin in their play. Wild birds nest in trees close to the cabin and are never bothered. Jimson does not have a cat; he likes the summer company of the birds more than the winter company of a cat. A lean hound dog shares his life. Living in the backwoods, Jimson is happy and contented. He asks only to be let alone to gather materials from the woods to make baskets in the cold months when he can't fish, hunt, and walk about the acres that surround him.

His wants are few: sugar, flour, extract, salt, pepper, soap, and tobacco in three forms—snuff, smoking and chewing. He dotes on having a Sears wish book for eyeball shopping only. He welcomes magazines for adding bright pictures to the walls of his already heavily papered cabin. Meal, meat, and potatoes he gets in return for baskets he makes for farmers about and around the countryside.

He also sells baskets that are made to order. If a housewife wants an egg basket made from white oak strips to hold ten dozen eggs, he will weave a flat-bottom basket with sturdy handle, which will hold ten dozen with a little leeway just in case the hens are laying big eggs.

Need a soiled-clothes basket with removable cover? This work of art will be less than two dollars, and he will make a nice whittled oak peg to fasten the top for one penny extra.

If you want a basket for the baby—one to take to the kitchen where the child can be near its mother—give him the size and time you want it. He will be happy to decorate the flat basket with rabbits or chicks in soft blue, yellow, or pink. Jimsom makes his dyes from flowers, bark, or herbs he gathers in the fields and woods from far and near.

The cotton baskets he weaves are works of art: flat-bottomed, with tapered sides and a rim that is strong enough to withstand countless cotton-picking seasons. For use in feeding animals around the barns, there is nothing better than a basket made by Jimson. He can make a basket that will hold ear corn for three horses out of seasoned white oak strips, with a standup handle to loop over your arm.

For keeping toys in their proper place after play, Jimson makes a flat basket with three-inch sides that will slip under the bed at night.

Yes, Jimson has a life that suits him. He has never seen a picture show, doesn't know what a pinup girl is, cares nothing for the state of the world. He reads his Bible each and every day, goes regularly to church, and believes all the pastor says. Such faith as his can only come to those who read, pray, and believe the Word.

He has various cousins who are always trying to get him to visit them in town and see the world. He wants nothing of it.

Each time I see him, with his long white hair, white beard, and clean but unironed clothes, coming to the mailbox or to get a gallon of skim milk, I think Oliver Goldsmith must have been thinking of Jimson Yarber when he wrote:

> His best companion, innocence
> and health,
> And his best riches, ignorance
> of wealth.

Calum Delse

C alum Delse lived a lonely life. To reach his few acres you had to cross Waggoner Creek, go past the red sand bed, and veer to the right, taking a dim narrow path through tangled brush and scrubby trees. At the back side of the upper place, you had to cross a marshy bog by stepping from stump to fallen log, and you hoped that a water snake would not fall on you from looped vines growing in the towering trees.

Mama and Grandmother Budd often sent Brother and me to take something to Calum—a mess of cropped collards, a pone of soda bread, a gallon bucket of clabber with a little pat of butter floating sweetly in the already wheying milk. Sometimes we took a paper cone filled with slips of yard flowers to be planted on his front fence line.

We had to call and hello until Calum shuffled to his front porch, or if that failed, we could pick up his conch shell and blow it three times. This shell was for friends only!

Calum had a flock of mean roosters roaming his property, as well as two hooking cows, a flock of butting goats, several biting dogs, a scratching cat, and two red-eyed hogs so long and lean they seemed like holy terrors to two small children on a mission of good will.

These animals were trained by Calum. He spoke and they did his bidding: the roosters were directed to take their places on gaunt limbs of a dead hickory nut tree, the cat jumped to his shoulder when he clapped his hands, and the goats lined up in pairs beside the fallen rail fence when he nodded his head. The biting dogs were under the high porch near the ground front room where they stayed until invited out with high keening wails, while the hooking cows were motioned to stand still by a shaking of Calum's right hand. All animals stood at attention. (I forgot the stomping mule, said to have gotten a neighbor's horse down and "done in" in a matter of minutes, stomped real good.)

We gave our goodies to this strange man with long hair and beard, accepted a few parched peanuts and a buckeye for each of us, and scooted homeward with anxious glances over our shoulders.

I was told he had a son out west and a daughter up north. My grandmother Budd said he never had a postcard from either. Every two weeks he came to the Budd home to see if he had any mail and to eat a good breakfast.

He raised a patch of cotton using the stomping mule to work it. When fall came and the cotton was gathered, the mule was hitched to a slide to bring the seed cotton to the big road, where a neighbor took it to the gin at Merwin. His crop was a few hundred pounds of cotton, and the few dollars it brought went to buy winter food: green coffee, beans, flour, a few pounds of rice, and a five-pound sack of sugar. The sugar lasted through the winter, for he used honey or molasses to sweeten his coffee and "pore folks' tea" until these farm sweeteners were used up.

Calum was afraid of strangers; he never invited a visitor to take a seat and talk. He would ask them what they wanted, ask for the time of day if the caller was known to carry a pocket watch, then go into his house and shut the door. The caller would hear the heavy cross-bar drop with a muffled thud.

When he died, his coffin was made by someone on Shady Rest and padded with cotton he had raised the year before and not sold. I thought it was awful to send him to his Maker resting on seed cotton. Grandmother and Aunt Phleta lined the coffin with black muslin tacked down with shiny galvanized tacks. They plumped up a porch pillow to rest his head on. He was dressed in his regular garb of skim milk-blue overalls and jumper to match. He had gone barefoot so long the new shoes (still in the box) could not be put on his feet, so they were put beside him in the coffin, as was the old brown coonskin cap that he wore day and night. Just before the coffin was closed, Grandmother put the cap on his head to make him look natural.

He was buried on his place under a tall tree. Those digging the grave had a time keeping the hooking cows, mean roosters, biting dogs, butting goats, stomping mule, long lean hogs with curving tusks, and scratching cat from taking over their efforts to get Calum Delse buried right and proper.

No one wanted the animals, as they were so old and out of control. They were left to fend for themselves on the rocky place. Brother and I never went that way again. The place grew up in bush and vines. After years had passed, a neighbor fenced the place and kept a few goats on it to eat the brush down.

Thinking about Calum reminded me of his favorite food: grits over rice. Grandmother would make this tasty dish on the day he came to see about his mail (that never came). If Grandmother had cheese, she would give him a small wedge to be chipped over the rice and grits combination. Buttered biscuits with blackberry jam was dessert.

Calum loved coffee. He was given an enameled cup filled to the brim with boiled coffee strong enough to float an egg. Grandmother never failed to say, "Calum, that coffee is going to give you the 'thumps,'" and his reply never varied, "Nome, it ain't never yet."

To my knowledge, he died never having had the "thumps." 🎴

Adeline Walker's Sit-in

In 1936 Adeline Walker, having heard that an Amite County welfare check was $8.50 more than the pauper stipend of $1.50 she received, asked my father Hiram Budd to apply for welfare in her name.

Adeline, who tipped the cotton gin scales at 300 pounds, was blind, had no teeth, confessed to not hearing well, and shuffled with slow steps even on her best days. She longed to make her mark on that magic paper, to be among the favorite few who eagerly awaited the mail carrier each first Monday of the month for a check.

When my father returned to Shady Rest farm, licking his wounds from the "set-to" with the welfare director, he told Adeline that there was no hope for a check for her. Adeline wanted to know what went on at the meeting where she was refused a check. My father told her the director had said, "Now, Budd, you keep on supporting Adeline. She worked for your in-laws for forty or more years."

Adeline, aged, fat, and blind but nobody's fool, said, "I want you to take me to the courthouse in Liberty and I'm gonner sit-in there until I get my check."

At five that summer afternoon, Bennie Jackson took Adeline, her chamber pot, a pone of cornbread, her palmetto fan, and a stone jug of water sweetened with molasses to the courthouse.

At that time there were long sturdy benches on the front porch.

(They are still there.) Adeline sat on one of the benches with her chamber pot underneath, jug and bread pone beside her, fan breezing her face when gnats came, a shawl around her shoulders, a man's brown felt hat pulled low on her brow, and a clay pipe clenched between trembling lips. She passed the night praying and singing soft songs to herself. She was watched over by Bennie, who had parked the truck across the street.

At good daylight the sheriff came to ask my father to come for Adeline, as the welfare director had agreed to put her on the rolls so she could get her check. 🈂

Aunt Elsie's Last Days

A reader writes: "I am now in my eighty-first year. I often awake in the night and recall the days of long ago; how my sickly mama took care of seven little children, "little stairsteps," she called us.

"My father worked away from home at a ground-hog sawmill one winter. He came home on Sundays, walking ten miles each way to be with his family a short time. When he arrived home he always made up the fire, then sat down down on the floor to play with us. I was the oldest, and Mama depended on me to help with the three youngest, ages one, two and three.

"While Mama was cooking dinner, Father cut splinters and split wood, which he stacked under the tall back porch, enough to see us through the coming week. He drew plenty of water for Mama to cook with and to bathe the children. There were barrels under the house eaves to catch rainwater to be used to wash clothes.

"One Sunday father said he wanted to talk to Mama about his only living relative, an aunt living in another county with her daughter-in-law, who had lost her mind and was being taken to the asylum next week by the law-and-order man.

"Mama thought about this matter all through dinner, then wondered where the old aunt would sleep. Father said, "She has a bed tick which needs to be emptied, as the hay is old and musty, a few quilts, a bedstead with no slats, a chamber pot, black iron skillet, and a grey speckled granite coffee pot which she told me made good coffee.

"Needless to say, Mama agreed. The next Sunday when Father came home, Aunt Elsie came to be with us. The law-and-order man sent the old woman to us riding in a buggy pulled by a lame, flop-eared, wall-eyed mule with no swishy tail. The emptied tick was stuffed in the back of the buggy, as were the few garments Aunt Elsie owned. Her coffee pot was in her lap, the chamber pot at her feet. We never saw the bedstead, and the quilts had been thrown away, for Father said they were filthy rags.

"Father stuffed the bed tick with hay and pinestraw. It was plumped up in one corner of the fireplace room with boards making a little pen to hold the floor-bed in place. How we loved to have a place to put the babies for naps on cold winter days.

"Aunt Elsie fit right in with our family. She was hard of hearing, going blind, and no trouble to feed. She wanted only gruel or mush at meal time, and coffee made fresh at least ten times a day. She wanted the water to be drawn fresh each time the coffee was made and the parched beans to be ground just before the coffee was boiled. After two weeks of coffee-making, Mama said, "No wonder Dorrie lost her mind. This coffee thing is driving me crazy."

"Our well was on the back porch. The water had to be pulled up by hand, as we had no windlass; how the pully whined and squeaked as Mama or I drew a bucket of fresh water. The coffee grinder was in the hall near the fireplace room.

"Mama came up with the idea of pulling a bit of rope through the pully to make it whine and turning the coffee grinder a few times so Aunt Elsie would think fresh coffee was being made. Mama made the granite pot full of coffee first thing in the morning and kept it hot in a boiler of water over the little eye on the cook stove. Aunt Elsie got hot coffee many times a day, but it was not as fresh as she thought.

"At the end of a year our aged aunt died. She had saved her pauper's check of $1.50 per month the whole time she was with us. Father was able to give her a nice funeral with the money. A coffin made by a neighbor cost $3.50 and a new dress was $1.95. There was a wreath of waxed flowers for her grave that cost over two dollars, which Aunt Elsie would have thought an outrageous price. Four dollars went to an old man who charged to dig graves, and who also whittled wooden grave markers with names and ages cut into the wood for two dollars.

"You ask what the rest of the pauper fund went for? Aunt Elsie drank it up in fresh coffee many times a day.

"Years later when I had married and had children of my own, we decided to look for her grave. I recalled a tall oak tree beside a pond near the graveyard. Imagine my surprise to find pastures where the graves had been. The pond was gone, as was the oak tree. Cows grazed on lush grass. When our children are gone, there will not be one person who remembers tales told about Aunt Elsie."

Daily Parades
and Other Adventures
on the Farm

A Right
Nice Grunt

Jack Sprat's pig,
He was not very little,
Nor yet very big.
He was not very lean,
He was not very fat.
He'll do well for a grunt
Says little Jack Sprat.

Old Nursery Rhyme

We have one of those pigs at our house—the runt of the litter. He is a sweet little fellow, so cunning and darling when he was a few hours old. Tiny and wrinkled, he looked ages old. His face had all the wonder and wisdom of pig-land etched in each wrinkle. The whole family fell in love with the smallest fellow of the brood.

There was no teat for him. We knew he would have to be hand fed or watched over to see that he wasn't pushed off each and every nursing time. Of course it was my job to listen for the mama hog when she felt her milk coming down. She would give a very satisfied series of grunts and fall over with a thud; then the piglets would go to work taking dinner in style.

Sometimes it would be impossible for me to drop something I was right in the middle of doing and play nursemaid. When I finally reached the nearby pen I would find the little fellow being a midget-sized tornado. He would race from one end of the row of nursing pigs to the other, then dash up onto the pile of pigs and vainly root and hunt for a place of his very own. Finding that he could not budge his larger littermates, he would go to his mother's head and nudge her, uttering plaintive piglet words, but to no avail.

Often I would find him stamping his pink hooves in dirt—man-sized stomps from hooves smaller than my middle fingernails. His tail had two curls that quivered with hunger and rage. He would run to me and begin touching my legs with his damp pink nose.

Reaching down, I would pluck a full fellow from the bosom of the mother, then gently place the runt in a warm spot for his share.

He lived but failed to grow. He looks like a very old man who has shrunk in size. His skin did grow some, and now it folds over the top of his back in ridges. He looks as if he has on socks that need pulling up. His eyes have kept their bright sparkle; the lashes curl and sweep up like a movie star's. Someone had the nerve to ask why we didn't get rid of our loved little pig, which we named Runt.

Dale answered that question with, "Well, now, I'll tell you why. We think he has a right nice grunt." 🐖

A Day
at the Fair

It is a funny thing about our son, Tim—though he is always eager to be first in most things, if he is the cow's tail in any event there is no use to worry. To his way of thinking just to be counted is enough. His very disposition is an asset; he is calm and placid and never in a hurry.

You take today: the Stevens family was going to the county fair. It was a day we had been looking forward to for many months.

We had sorted and re-sorted the various farm products for our choicest and best of everything. Only this morning we had pulled the big pumpkin over in the cornfield, having let it grow until the very last minute. It was a fine fat fellow, sure to win first prize, for it tipped the scales at forty-five pounds.

Peanuts had been picked from the several bushels raised on Shady Rest. Pecans were lovingly polished with a soft cloth to bring out the perfect sheen on the beautiful Stuarts that came from trees planted some years ago.

Garden vegetables had been gathered while the dew decked them with jewels of sheer beauty: peppers green as emeralds, fall tomatoes blushed with vivid ruby tones, and snapbeans as slender as polished pencils, tenderly green and gently curved on the ends. Fall squash, both white and yellow, nestled in a bed of parsley, smart and modern looking as next year's paint. Irish potatoes turned pale red faces to the early sun as they were routed from snug beds in the last row of the garden; gently washed under the garden hose, they seemed ready for a blue ribbon.

My part had been to sort and carefully pick over the loot from the Stevens's pantry so as to get the finest jar of each vegetable and fruit listed in the catalogue from the fair officials. There were seven kinds of jelly: peach, plum, blackberry, grape, apple, mayhaw, and strawberry, all nestled in a cottonseed-filled box along with various jams and jewel-toned relishes.

The livestock grew impatient, waiting in the truck. The hens grew fussy and began to dress their feathers, which had been carefully brushed and touched with oil before the sun was up.

The prize cow mooed gently and lovingly to her calf. She began to lick his coat this way and that, with long happy swipes of her tongue. Horrified, I saw an hour's work vanish in a few licks. Where only a blink and wink before, slick wavy hair had shown like satin, now there were cowlicks every-which-way on Sandy!

Fat piglets began to think longingly of clabber and boiled corn and added their shrill squeals to the already tense atmosphere.

Where was Tim, the youngest child going to the fair, and the one who owned or claimed all the hens on our yard? Of course we used the eggs, and I sold the extra ones to buy things for the family: raisins, marshmallows for toasting and hot chocolate, corn flakes, crackers, icing sugar, brown sugar, and picture show tickets—things the farm didn't provide.

Looking around, I saw eleven eggs on the porch table—eggs picked out to take to the fair, the biggest and best our white leghorn hens could produce—eleven eggs when the fair rules clearly stated twelve. Eleven eggs and no Tim!

Sudden insight came my way, and I went to the hen house to look for our son. Sure enough, there was Tim, sitting in the midst of forty hens, over half of them on the nest. When I asked him what he was doing, he said, "Well, Meme, when I weighed those eggs last night, the ones I had to pick from were just a bit of weight off. I'm waiting for the hens to lay. Out of that many eggs, I can find one to make a perfect dozen."

What did we do? We waited until Gay Breeze, Butterfly, Dew Drop, and Daisy, along with other sisters of the flock, laid the perfect egg to finish out the dozen destined for the Amite County Fair.

After we reached the fairgrounds, I began sorting out the sewing, garden sass and canned things, displaying them to advantage. Dale and Joe were tending the livestock and putting more waves on the calf, Sandy. Tim slipped away to borrow a horse to ride in the parade to be held at twelve noon.

We had our share of white and red ribbons. Tim's perfect dozen white leghorn eggs won a blue ribbon and, to ice the cake, also won the overall purple ribbon for the special 4-H Club eggs. 🔳

Holding
Buddy Over

M any years ago farmers often "carried" a hog over from one winter to the next, thereby hoping to grow a "lard hog." In the early years of our marriage, it was my decision to take a hog over from one early October to the next October.

Buddy was a big hog when the decision was made. By early spring he had grown so large that a bigger pen had to be built. The new pen, built under a lovely water oak, was made of peeled pine poles and floored with thick oak planks. A trough ran from one side of the pen to the other; Buddy was a big eater. If the trough was allowed to get dry, he kept up a constant refrain. Coming from a hog as large as Buddy, this noise soon got on a person's nerves.

Two barrels of soured wheat or rice shorts were kept going at all times for Buddy's pleasure. Shucked corn was thrown over into the pen, not by the dozen but by the basketful.

At that time we had no electricity, hence no running water; all water had to be drawn from a deep well. Of course I saved every drop of dishwater, along with bath water, for the hog. A slop can (the bane of a housewife) was duly installed in my kitchen.

As summer came across the land, people came on Sundays to see Buddy. Men stood around the pen, discussing and wondering if Buddy would reach 800 pounds by the first hard freeze. That summer not one peach, plum, pear, nor apple went to waste. The children were determined to make a real one-of-a-kind hog to show off and in the end dress him out as the largest hog raised in Amite County.

I was expecting Rose, Jr., in October. The smells from the Buddy pen were almost beyond endurance. I grant you it wasn't a steady smell, but if the wind was just right you knew something was almost rotten below the little barn. When I'd voice a complaint about the smell, Dale or one of our sons would take a deep breath and say, "Man, man, just smell that lard, pork chops, ham and chitterlings."

August came and went; September days were hot and brassy; October came with sunny mild days and very light frosts. It would take a billy-goat-horn-freezing snap to do justice to Buddy's heavy hams. Still he waxed fat and fatter. He no longer grunted his way from pen corner to trough; he sat there waiting for food. Long ago his eyes had vanished under layers of gobby fat.

Indeed, he had eaten through two corn crops, and if cold weather didn't hurry, it seemed as if we would have him on our hands for another year.

Finally a freezing wind promised cold. The battery radio gave warning of "heavy frost with a sharp drop in temperature to around twenty-two degrees."

October twenty-first was the day neighbors gathered to help dress out Buddy—make lard, turn chitterlings, mold head cheese, grind sausage meat, and salt down the hams, shoulders and bacon sides.

At weighing time I went to the hospital to deliver our daughter, Rose, Jr. Dale wanted to know if I could hang around until Buddy was weighed. Outsiders marked Buddy's weight at 738 pounds, a figure Dale and our sons never believed. They had estimated 850 pounds.

Nobody at our house would touch the meat from Buddy. Biscuits and pie crusts made with his lard were shunned, sausage went begging, the hams hung for two years before we gave them away. In fact, we gave every last crumb of Buddy away to friends and neighbors, who pronounced it excellent! 🈸

Orphans
on the Farm

B aby chicks are cute and cunning anytime; however, I can't think of anything more likely to throw a household into confusion than eleven biddies. These were found on a sparkling frosty morning in January.

My breath, as well as the snorts of the milk cows, made fluffy plumes in the cold morning air. Grass was slippery with frost. I was in the process of driving the dry cows from the barn to the pasture.

The path was deep, pocked and spewed with ribbon ice. The lead cow shied and tossed her head, her horns sparkling in the early morning sun. She went galloping across the pasture away from the open gap, leading the other two cows to follow her gamboling way.

Wondering what had caused this sudden flurry of extra energy, I took a careful look directly in front, where the lead cow had been when she seemed to be scared out of her wits. I stood with my mouth agape, looking at a seemingly just-hatched fluffy yellow chick. It regarded me with a black-eyed stare, liked what it saw, and began to slip and slide toward me, finally falling into a deep cow track. My jacket pocket made a cozy nest for this 'lorn and lost baby, as I rounded up the cows and drove them through the gap.

I had an Easter hunt in January, finding five little fellows beside the path, huddled under tall frosted grass. Four more were in the nest a hen had stolen, under a tangled clump of berry briars. There was a pipped egg in the nest, complete with a struggling chick.

The pipped egg was placed in a cotton-lined box in the warming oven of the stove. The ten biddies were made snug in a wooden shell box with fine oatmeal and warm water for refreshments.

After tending the babies, I went looking for the mother of these youngsters. Seven of the dozen hens we keep to give us "nest pearls" already were settled deep in their pinestraw-filled nests. Questioning the five that were eating laying mash did no good—not one would admit to being the mother of the brood in my care. Careful examination showed no bare spots on their breasts, a usual sign of having stayed on a nest of eggs for twenty-one days.

Evidently the mother of my chicks must have wandered from a neighbor's and set up housekeeping below our barn. A pitiful pile of feathers found a day later bore out my belief; a fox, wild cat, or skunk had made a meal of the hapless hen during the night before my find.

Everything should be peaches and cream around here with chicks to tend, a Boston Terrier all proper and queen of the house, and a pallet for the black tom cat. There is some dispute! The cat stalks around with tail fluffed twice its natural size, passing the chick box with hisses that seem to spit ill will at the motherless biddies.

Lady, the Boston, barks and barks until I am ready to nominate her for the biggest-coward-in-the-world award. When I put a chick on the floor in front of her, all the bark is gone and the heretofore brave Boston backs away and slinks under the bed or table, whimpering.

Dale is trying to make up his mind which is more nerve-racking: a Boston barking at a chick not much bigger than two thumbs put together, or that same dog looking out the window on a cold night and baying at the moon.

Tomorrow we will have the electric brooder ready for the chicks, none too soon for Dale and me. I am sure Lady and the tom cat will rejoice when things are back to normal where they rule the roost, so to speak.

Screech Owl Warnings

First the sound was deep in the woods near the sheep pasture branch—a sound so bloodchilling that it sent goose bumps up the arm I had out from under the light sheet needed for cover in early morning after midnight.

This seems to be a favorite time for these small feathered creatures to send out their messages, said by the old folk in my pre-salad days to be warnings of death or bad happenings. There might be a message to tell people to start doing better or watch out!

I can remember Uncle Burrel Taylor coming to my father's house on a nippy fall morning to ask my father if he had heard the screech owls in the little woods below the old lake.

If my father had heard the owls, he pretended to have slept like a log, knowing full well the aged, bearded man wanted to tell, once again, of the dire happenings to loved ones, and best of all, to those he bore grudges against. The old man would take a blue granite cup filled with fresh coffee that was sweetened with rock sugar from the bottom of an empty syrup can, put his feet into ashes spilling from the just-built fire, and begin.

Did my father recall when Fred had a hex put on him minutes after a screech owl called, and a tree was struck by lightning, killing all three of his cows that were under it?

Remember the unfortunate baby born to the folks living across Pearl Branch, how the baby never cried or squalled like a normal baby, just screeched, like an owl had done about an hour before the baby was born?

Did my father recall the time when a wagon had been loaded with seed cotton, well tromped down and ready for the road to the gin—didn't Louis miss his step when he was swinging up to drive the mules and wagon to the gin, breaking his jaw? In pain and anger didn't he whip the mules, causing them to run away and turn the wagon off the bridge into the deep water at the old mill tail?

Wasn't it bad, bad when little Froanie was bitten by a snake and swelled up like a toad frog, how her maw killed one hen at a time to put the bitten foot inside the hen to draw out the snake venom? Here was a family without hens to lay and the child died anyway.

All these things happened, Uncle Burrel maintained, because those hearing the screech owls didn't believe the tried-and-true rules of warding off the bad luck sure to be caused by those pesky screech owl calls.

I put my arm under the cover and listened several minutes, enjoying the calling and answering of owls. Then I slipped out of bed to go into the kitchen, where I turned my apron pockets wrong side out. I took towels and covered all the mirrors in the house, even remembering to turn the face mirror over. (That mirror is so old the silver is flaking from the back. When I look at myself in it, I am careful to remember that I am not really so spotted—I shut one eye and make do. Why do I keep such a mirror? It is very old and well-loved, and the back is beautiful.)

Many nights when Tim, our middle child, would hear the high quivering call of the very small owls, he would come to creep into bed with Dale and me. He would also help turn pockets wrong side out and scurry about with towels for me to drape over mirrors.

To Tim's delight he once found and brought home a tiny little screech owl that had fallen from a nest deep in the Old Lake thicketwoods. It gave tiny, tiny litle screeches we didn't feel would cause bad luck. Within a few days, it faded away and died, which Tim pointed out was our fault for not covering mirrors and turning out pockets. 🏵

Going for a Setting of Eggs

The setting of a broody hen is fun. Who can resist putting cottonseed in the bottom of an eight-pound lard bucket, then carefully placing sixteen eggs there, and adding more seed to cover?

On the day we go off to get a setting of eggs, Rose, Jr., our youngest child, hunts for her bonnet. She comes out wearing the coontail cap belonging to Joe, her oldest brother, explaining that her bonnet wasn't where it was supposed to be, and anyway she doesn't mind a few new freckles.

A walk down a country road is always a pleasure. I start out with firm sure strides, promising to be back home in just over two hours.

Rose, Jr., discovers sheep sorrel growing on the side of a tall bank. How sharp and tingly it feels to our tongues. The juice is sweetly sour as we chew the leaves. I realize that childhood is always the same; my daughter is following right where I trod years ago.

The perfection of a clump of dog-tooth violets must be examined and a few gathered to pull through a buttonhole in my dress. Red lilies are blooming at the burnt house (where Dale was badly burned in April, 1946, when he saved Adeline Walker's life). I examine the peach trees at the house site and note a goodly crop, lovely clingstone peaches that make the best whole preserves in the world.

I note, with interest, martins swooping and flying above the martin house in Zeb Freeman's back yard, too many martins for his box. I invite the extra ones to come to our new martin house that Dale built last week; our swinging line of gourds is waiting for martins to come and stay.

When we reach Waggoner Creek bridge, Rose, Jr., runs ahead

and drops on all fours to peer between the cracks of the bridge flooring. Why the water looks more exciting when seen through cracks, I don't know. She calls in excited voice to come see the mama fish swimming around a circle of rocks. I explain that the fish is guarding her eggs. Suddenly, from tall reeds a jack fish darts out and tries to scare the mama fish away, then turns tail and goes to happier hunting grounds. We gather rocks to throw with satisfying plunks into the water of the old mill tail where a cotton gin was long ago. How large the splashes are. We look at each other in glee and hurry over the bridge, for we hear a car coming.

In the bend of the road we stop and press against a huge honeysuckle bush, waiting for the car to pass. The scent of pink and white flowers is almost overpowering. The air is filled with the drone of honey bees. The car gets to us and comes to a stop. It's a new car, bright red, with a nice-looking man who wants to know if we have gold to sell—watches, rings, old gold bridge work, fancy pins, belt buckles. I say, "No, our New Orleans aunt tends to business for us." Then he says, "Well, you have a mighty pretty little girl and you ain't such a bad-looking doll yourself."

I feel Rose, Jr., stiffen against me as the car moves on. She slips her hand into mine and says, "That man must not know you are Pa's wife."

We come to the old Gene House. Little calves are busy rubbing their heads against fence posts, easing the itch where little horns are growing. I show Rose, Jr., how to push the hair aside and rub the knobby horns. The little fellows love our attention; some butt heads and fling themselves about, putting on a show for us. Mama cows stroll to the fence and stick inquiring noses through. A handful of grass is eaten with relish, even though the clover on their side is knee deep.

We skirt a few mud puddles, cross a foot log at Agnes Branch, make our way across a grassy old field bottom filled with crayfish houses, each one made with mud balls—works of art to a crayfish.

We reach the house where Cassie Sojourner is waiting for us. She tells us she saw us coming down the road well before we reached the creek. For years we have gone for a setting of frizzle hen eggs, hoping to be proud owners of at least a dozen chickens with their feathers growing the wrong way (every feather on a frizzle chicken grows backward and does not lie flat but curls up). Several times we have hatched frizzled biddies. Even though such chickens are supposed to bring good luck, we never had much luck raising them to grown hens. An owl got one, the hog ate three, a woods cat helped himself to one, I stepped on one, and the others went away.

Cassie invites us to have a seat on the front porch, while she goes to the back porch to swap out the eggs. She reminds me not to put the eggs under the setting hen until twenty-four hours have passed— something about letting the yolks settle.

Rose, Jr., asks if she can go in the front room and admire the mantle cloth, which is made from paper. Cassie asks if we would like such a mantle cloth and what design we would like her to cut. I lean toward moons and stars. Rose, Jr., asks for Washington crossing the Delaware. Cassie informs us that she has never heard of either and will cut to please herself; she keeps patterns in her mind.

Newspaper is folded many times. Cassie cuts, slashes, and turns the paper. She cuts with a very sharp razor, the kind you strop on a razor strop to get keen fine edges. With scissors, she makes a nice fringe across the bottom of the pretty she has made. Unfolded, her pleasure is a flag with stars in the upper left-hand corner.

We take our leave, inviting Cassie to come visit us soon. When we reach the big road, we overtake Kyle Green, who offers us a ride on his homemade slide, pulled by one of his blind oxen. There isn't much room, as he is taking a bushel of shelled velvet beans to Uncle Ben to swap for shoe-peg corn seed. I walk, and Rose, Jr., rides, being careful not to mash a paper cone filled with flower cuttings Leathie is sending Uncle Ben's wife, Mae. (In those days, much was made over neighbors sending things to neighbors when swaps were made.) I ask Kyle if he knows what he will be asking for Leathie in the swap. He allows he doesn't know, although Leathie is leaning toward cuttings of angel wing begonia and feather plume grass.

When we reach home, the school bus stops to deliver our sons, Joe and Tim. They want to hear about our day of fun and frolic, saying to Rose, Jr., that she better enjoy her time now when she doesn't have to wear shoes and keep her hair combed, doesn't have to learn times tables, and doesn't have girls try to kiss you when you play games the teachers have selected.

These delightful days will never come again. I want my daughter to remember her childhood with delight and pleasure, not as a time of hurrying here and scurrying there. ▨

The Blessings
of Memory

Have you longed to relive a week, month or day of your life? If you have fallen into such a trap, what was the scene, scent, or memory that brought this throat thickening, eye stinging, heart yearning to full bloom?

This very morning it became necessary for me to journey to a distant part of our county, traveling by paved road, turning off on a gravel road, thence to a dirt road, and next following a private winding road completely carpeted with pinestraw until I had to walk along a path wide enough only for one person. Turning a corner, I came upon an open field being plowed by a lad who looked to be about ten years of age. A beautiful scene: the sun was shining, birds were hopping behind the turning earth, pecking at goodies—worms, grubs, and tender roots.

All at once I felt as if time had snapped into the past, April 1949. I felt a kinship with the lad plowing. How proudly he held the handles of the plow that were entirely too large for his slight size. He gave the proper words of "gee" and "haw" to the animal pulling the plow. I had a strong desire to go to the child and look him in the face, hoping to see the man he dreamed of being in twenty years. To my left I noticed a much smaller boy coming across the still-to-be-plowed rows, carrying a bucket that sloshed water with every uneven staggering step he took, his progress slowed greatly by the baby he was carrying. The wee child on his back bobbed up and down, clasping her chubby hands tightly around the little boy's neck, her legs around his waist. Why should my heart lurch, eyes fill with tears, throat thicken to the point the ache was almost unbearable? I had to restrain myself from running to these children and asking, "Do I know you, do you remember me? Would you like to go on a picnic when you finish out the row?" If I had given in to my feelings, I am sure the middle child would have turned his liquid brown eyes to my face and said, "What do you have good to eat in the basket? Buttered biscuits with plenty of sugar or jelly, carrots and lettuce leaves, milk in pop bottles to put in the branch to cool until time to eat?"

What was it in this scene that tricked me? Not the children, for they were of another race. Then I knew: the oldest child was plowing with a donkey, and alongside trotted a baby donkey nipping at its mother, turning every few steps to direct playful kicks toward her, trying to sip a few drops of milk from her strutting bag.

APRIL 1949. The morning was just right for plowing. Joe, our oldest son, was going alone on his first sortie into the world of grownups. He hitched Emma, the mama donkey, to a plow with handles too high for him. In vain he tried to shut the donkey's three-month-old baby in a pen. After Joe had been gone about an hour, Tim left, taking a bucket of water to the field. Rose, Jr., cried to go and Tim rode her piggyback, telling her to hold him tight around the neck. I promised to follow with goodies in a basket—milk in pop bottles to cool in Agnes Branch, buttered biscuits (some with sugar, some with jelly), lettuce leaves, and little carrots.

The field my father gave our sons to tend was near the upper place (so called because it was on a hillside above the home place), reached by a narrow path carpeted with pinestraw, thickly crowded by woods. A turn and there was the field—Joe plowing, Tim staggering across unplowed rows, water sloshing, with Rose, Jr., about to choke him, Emma, the mother donkey, and her mouse-colored baby nipping and nuzzling her for sips of milk. The day Joe and Tim planted their field was a calm unhurried picture I thought I'd never forget. But I did forget in the almost twenty years that passed how our sons planted popcorn, okra, peanuts, and watermelons. The rows were nice and well plowed with barnyard fertilizer to enrich the ground, and Dale and I hoped every peanut would produce preacher nuts (three to every shell).

Have you had such a flashback, one that left you feeling blessed to remember it? If you have, share it with a good friend. 🈁

The Little Orchard

D o you have a special little place near where you live, a spot so loved by your children that they will remember it when they are grown and gone from home? Our children remember, and I, too, like to recall the wonderful days they spent in play in the "little orchard."

Down in the little orchard, oxeye daisies grow in a solid sheet close by the small water hole. When they are in bloom, the area looks as if a yellow and white carpet has been spread. Nestled beneath the oxeyes are several varieties of small yellow flowers, tiny stars-of-earth. Blue field daisies add a border around the yellow blooms, reflecting the blue sky. On the fence grow yellow and pink honeysuckle, and red rambling roses bloom constantly during summer months.

In one corner of the patch is a bank of red plum trees, short stubby fellows, which my mother said were bearing when she came to Shady Rest as a bride. There are also yellow plum trees, two white peach trees, a red clingstone peach so old the peaches are knotty when ripe, and two ancient green apple trees (they have never given us apples, even after bearing glorious drifts of blooms visited by bees for sweet nectar). A quince tree is always loaded with hard green quince that never reach full size, as the children cannot resist eating the mouth-twisting sour fruit with cow salt. Most wonderful of all, there is a pear tree growing up and up with two limbs down low for small children to climb.

This almost-an-acre is an enchanted place, fenced on all sides. This is where the baby calves are put when they first leave their mothers. How these semi-babies love to run and play in the big free place. They sniff the water hole, drawing back with turned-up lips when they discover the water isn't rich creamy milk. The water is teeming with wiggly-tailed fellows known as tadpoles.

A turkey nest is under the rosebushes growing on the fences. The children feel of great importance when they come to the house to say that "Fussy Mama" has a nest with twelve eggs in it. Twelve eggs never produce that many poults. Wandering dogs, foxes, and skunks eat their share, often leaving the mourning hen with no eggs at all.

The children make forts and playhouses and climb trees. They muddy around the edges of the water hole, hoping for a hand-sized perch. They are happy with wee mud cats about finger length. They string the floppy fellows on a forked limb to bring to the house to show Grandmother Budd and me; then the mudcats are turned loose in the water hole to be caught on the morrow.

When the school bus comes in the afternoon, the calves begin to romp and play, flinging themselves high in the air, tossing their tails about, seeming to invite our sons for a romp. They run to the fence and rub their knobby heads (soon there will be little horns where the hair-covered knobs are) against the prick of the sharp barbed wire. The calves will stand still when Tim rubs their faces, talking the while to the little fellows about how sweet they are.

The little orchard brings in nothing to help fill the family purse. Instead it gives pleasure and fills the heart with joy. A crib of corn could never take the place of even one hour of our children's play in the little orchard. 🔳

Emma's Quest

Emma the donkey came aboard at Shady Rest when our first-born was around six years of age. The owner failed to tell my father that Emma was a May-born baby. Emma had made things on his farm a sort of jumble as she naturally drifted toward water— pond, branch, creek, dipping vat, even deep mud holes and pasture hog wallows. All were a delight to Emma. It seemed as if his women-folk couldn't draw water to pour in big zinc tubs for clothes washing.

This information came out when my father went to see the man who had sold Emma to him. When Daddy asked Mr. Ellis why he hadn't told him the donkey was a May-born, to his credit the former owner replied, "Well, I had a sneaking idea you wouldn't have bought her. My womenfolks said it was either them or Emma when she had snaggered their wash water for the fifth time, turning the tubs over and stomping them in."

Daddy knew when he was snookered. He came home and gave

instructions to keep all gates shut, tubs emptied, and the door to the dipping vat closed. He hoped thereby to keep Emma from water where she could splash, wallow, and swim if the water was deep enough. It didn't work. There were many workers on Shady Rest who had chores to do with rules to be followed, and tending the donkey was extra. No matter if a gap or gate was tied with wire or rope—Emma was adept when it came to nuzzling latches open. Those tied with rope didn't stand a chance, as she would patiently gnaw the rope if there was water on the other side.

You see, there were Agnes Branch, Pearl Branch, Old Field Branch, Waggoner Creek, Old Lake Branch, and hog wallows in three pastures, all calling to the something in her breast. Somewhere in her makeup the words "running water" had been imprinted. Mayborn colts are partial to running water. Emma liked it any way—shallow, running, deep, or fast.

When our sons grew to be trusted with Emma for riding or pulling a homemade slide, things picked up. Two little boys were often left beside the road when Emma decided she wanted to get to water.

Many were the times in summer when the field hands were at the barn getting their mules ready for an afternoon of work when there would be much calling and yahooing to say, "Emma is out and headed for the creek." Dogs would start barking and running after Emma. As they passed houses on the way, other dogs would run from under the houses, joining in the uproar and parade. When the path to the old mill tail was reached, Emma made a beeline for the deep end, giving a little dance-step before she soared out, landing in the water with the dogs paddling behind.

Once an old woods rooster was picking about in weedy mud near the creek bank when Emma and the dogs passed by. In sudden fright, the rooster flew directly from the bank to Emma's back, where he balanced, wings flapping, until the swimming, braying, barking kit-and-caboodle reached the other side.

Our sons were elated to know there was a circus on Shady Rest. Unfortunately, this special event never happened again, no matter how they watched and waited for the rooster to repeat his bareback ride.

The Daily Parade at Shady Rest

A nice welcome is always enjoyed, especially when it is sincere and is given without the expectation of anything in return.

Every afternoon when I go into the freezer house to get feed for the laying hens, I am greeted by mama cat who has climbed on the window sill to get away from her kittens. The minute I open the screen door she gets up, and I firmly believe she gives me a snaggled-toothed smile—at least it looks that way to me. She stretches, gives a few licks to her white chest fur, then settles down to enjoy a rub behind her ears and praise for her three well-behaved kittens who do not scratch my feet and legs, nor whine and meow for milk or food. The three kittens are beautiful creatures: one solid black, one grey-and-black striped, the other pure white. Mama cat is grey-and-black striped.

We have visiting toms; one is a black knight gliding from shadow to shadow on moonlit nights. Another is a white tom, a lovely ghost as he sits on a fence post making the night shiver with his tales of love in a high screeching voice.

Sometime I get amused at the parade that takes place each afternoon when Dale and I go to the barn to finish up the night chores. As is fitting, the man of the house goes first with a bucket of broken fresh corncobs to put in the trough along with a few shucks, cottonseed meal, and pea hulls for the milk cow to enjoy while she is being milked.

I come next with the sparkling clean milk bucket. Behind me come two or three bantam chickens, mama cat and her kittens. All we need is a fife, drum, and American flag to have our own parade.

When Dale begins to milk, I stand by to hold the cow's tail (she packs a mean wallop when the tail is loaded with cockleburs). The bantams wait with impatience for me to slap horse flies to the ground; they gobble them up quick as a wink.

Mama cat and her kittens love warm milk direct from the cow and sit in a row waiting for Dale to squirt arches of milk their way. When they have enjoyed splashes of milk on their faces, they at once begin to groom themselves so that their appearance will befit Shady Rest cats.

The calf is let into its mother's stall to finish off the one teat

Dale has left him.

I go by the clothesline to get the strainer cloth for the milk. In the kitchen I skim a crock of clabber, put the cream in "the blue bowl," turn the clabber into a flour sack, and take the sacked clabber outside to drip. There will be cottage cheese for breakfast.

This summer treat is delicious when served with sliced peaches and sourdough biscuits. Our visiting New Orleans aunt wanted her daily dish of cottage cheese sprinkled with brown sugar and flooded with fresh warm milk.

If you are of the school to drip your own cheese, be sure to put a pan under the dripping sack to catch the whey for the little pig. They say whey is filled with good things for your health. Surely a little pig would wax fat on milk and whey.

From Conveniences to Gadgets

M any years ago I wrote: Water does the running on our farm now! We have electricity coming from over hill and dale to Shady Rest. The well wheel has ground out its last squeak, and the path to the creek has grown over with tall weeds and grass. You see, we once took our laundry to the creek, in the warm months.

How easy it was to dip water from the blue hole to fill three zinc tubs with cool creek water when it was time to rinse out the rest of the handboard-rubbed things. I used homemade lye soap and bought blueing for extra-white clothes these long years ago. Once rinsed, the clothing was draped over low-growing bushes to dry in the summer sun.

While I washed, the children played in the shallows, making rainbows when they threw water into the air. They tried to dam up the creek with sand carried in their little buckets from a sand bank. (Being little fellows, they were not bothered by the uselessness of this effort.)

We took a lunch of leftover breakfast biscuits with butter and jelly or jam inside, yesterday's baked sweet potatoes warmed in ashes around the wash pot, and fried fish. It all tasted delicious when eaten in the shade of tall trees.

When the clothes were dry and folded, the children were bathed and dressed in fresh clothes smelling of sunshine. We spread a sheet under the shade of a spice bush for delicious little naps.

The clothes were loaded into the wheelbarrow. Rose, Jr., took her seat in the little red wagon, and away we went to the house after a day of fun, food and play. Washing machines put an end to these adventures.

No longer did we depend on the rain barrels under house eaves to catch rainwater. (The water that came from these big oak barrels banded with iron always tasted faintly of whiskey.)

The coming of electricity also did away with the coming of the ice truck. No longer did housewives wrap a block of ice in old quilts or newspapers or bury the ice in a wooden box filled with sawdust or cottonseed. Both kept ice well for several days, if no chipping was allowed. Food put in half-gallon jars buried beside the ice could be kept from spoiling. If there was a good-sized chunk of ice and company came, how special it was to offer them fresh lemonade.

My mother loved her electric ice box! It was hard to remember to call the snow-white beauty a refrigerator. The blessing of "having cold" day and night was beyond price.

Being able to take a bath in a tub long enough to sit down in amazed many old folk who had never seen such; nor had they seen an iron that did not have to be heated at the fireplace. Gone were the days of "airing out" clothes worn to church so they could be worn again on the first Sunday of the next month.

One old gentleman never got used to having his pancakes made with criss-cross markings—a waffle iron was something used by town folks only. His dear wife would not use an electric heating pad except to put in a box to keep baby chicks warm. She would take a chunk from the back of the fireplace, sprinkle it down with water, and wrap it in newspapers and a piece of old army blanket left over from World War I. She took this to bed to comfort her aching back.

Their town children continued to give their aged parents every electric gadget on the market. Some the old folks unwrapped, wondered what in the world to do with, then stuck under their spare room bed. Others they displayed on their sideboard: an electric back scratcher, a can opener, an egg boiler, and a coiled wire said to heat up a cup of water for coffee.

They sure didn't think much of the last-mentioned gadget. These old dears made a big pot of coffee first thing in the morning: coffee tied in a rag, put in a granite coffee pot filled with fresh well water, then boiled and boiled, cleared with crushed egg shells, sweetened with molasses, and clouded with a smidgen of sweet cream.

Dale never liked ice cream made in a refrigerator. We continued to buy fifty pounds of ice when we wanted to make hand-turned cream, and we would make a party of the getting ready for the turning of the freezer. Best of all, the children got to lick the dasher. 🔳

Poor Maude

During the second spring after Pearl Harbor, Dale and I lived in Alabama and had rooms in the home of Mrs. Powers, who certainly must have been a "good woman" as the term goes, for she opened her house to wives of servicemen and to families who had jobs at nearby camps.

Her prices were reasonable. However, had I known that Mrs. Powers's tongue was tied in the middle and loose on both ends I would have pitched a tent (no matter how dotted with holes the top was) under a thorn bush or, better still, crept into one of the numerous caves found in the hills outside the small village where we lived.

I heard about Edd's wife, who was the daughter-in-law of Mrs. Powers, from coffee to gravy—that is, from breakfast to supper!

The others who lived in her home worked, so I was left to listen to a mother-in-law who gave tongue to the slipshod ways of "that good-for-nothing-lazy Maude" from daylight until well after dark, any day all day and double time on weekends. Then the working women were captive victims of her talk as they did their wash or baked a cake in the Powers's kitchen, taking advantage of their kitchen privileges for an hour or so.

Where most daughters-in-law are made out to be all wool and a yard wide, not so with Maude; she was as stringy and no-account as a bar of soap after a big wash day! She had no get-up-and-go, no spunk, no "kat-a-zam" (I never found out what that one was). She was the most awful cook in the world and fed Edd's children food from tin cans and bleached flour bread bought at the store. (I thought for quite sometime the children were Edd's by another wife—not so, they belonged to Edd and Maude, only she got no credit for their being in this world.)

Mrs. Powers would tell me twice a day (as I struggled to cook for three people on a one-burner oil stove) how her son Edd's wife never made a biscuit but bought them by the can. Did I know the lazy thing rolled the biscuits thin and cut them in strips to make dumplings for chicken pies? She even thought nothing about poking her finger through a flattened biscuit, frying it in deep fat, and calling it a doughnut. (The canned biscuit hints for dumplings and doughnuts were two of the best cooking hints I learned during the war; in fact, I still use both of them.)

It mattered not that Edd and his children cooked these same goodies for themselves while Maude worked ten hours per day to help pay off a big hospital bill run up by Mrs. Powers's long-gone-to-his-reward husband. I found out months later that Mr. Powers wasn't Edd's father—only a stepfather and uncle!

Mrs. Powers predicted Edd would die in the "pore house" and it would be the fault of that lazy wife of his.

Everytime Mrs. Powers did anything in a saving mood, she at once began to berate and fuss about Maude. Once when she was at her sewing machine sewing up a run in a silk stocking, all the while patting herself on the back for being so saving, she said, "That lazy wife of Edd's will wear stockings with so many runs they look like spider webs. She won't take time to stitch up the runs." I didn't wonder at Maude, for the sewing machine-sewed runs were lumpy and looked awful.

Every Saturday, the faraway Maude would have more sins trotted out, and we had to listen. Did we know Maude was going to put Edd in the pore house? She thought nothing about putting starched and ironed clothes on every one of Edd's children every day—changed their clothes from skin out every day, was wearing them out washing them. She even let Edd's children wear their Sunday shoes on Saturday when the family went grocery shopping.

Seems as if Edd and his family farmed on the side. Maude refused to make sheets using fertilizer sacks—not as long as she could afford ninety cents for a sheet.

The last thing I heard about Maude and her shiftless ways was one day when I was trying to get the feathers off a stewing hen. The water hadn't been hot enough, and the skin began to tear as I pulled on the feathers. Muttering to myself, I said, "I believe I'll skin this old hen and be done with her."

Guess what? Mrs. Powers spoke up and said, "You are getting to be just like Edd's wife—why, she thinks nothing of skinning chickens, says Edd's children don't like skin on their chickens. Anybody knows the best nourishment is under the skin. Yes indeed, pore house here comes Edd." 🏮

A Day to Remember

R ain fell in the night with a gentle swish, so softly the ground drank every drop. At sunrise the whole world began to sparkle and glitter. Red clover in the field above the house glowed and rippled in a soft little wind that came whispering over the pines. Over in the west field, cotton and corn showed bravely green—straight rows of cotton and gently curving rows of corn—promises of plenty and more to spare come fall.

Soon the house is cleaned, the children's clothes are starched and ironed and ready for two little boys and one little girl going to Sunday school. Rose, Jr.'s, sash ties in a sweet bow at first try. Dale looks the proud part of husband and of father to three children.

The boys are snaggled of tooth, freckled of nose, and cowlicked of hair. The mother flies around prodding and prompting so her little family will be on time.

When I am old and see through a glass darkly, when these faint wrinkles I have now multiply and deepen, when these hands now steady tremble and slop things over the fresh tablecloth my daughter-in-law has just ironed, when every step that passes my door is awaited with a longing heart that someone is coming to listen to me—dear Lord, please let me always remember this Sunday. 🏮

Tim's Loving Heart

O ur youngest son Tim has love in his heart for every person, with absolutely no conception of racial prejudice, as well as love for every other living creature.

Here at Shady Rest he wants to keep every dog, cat, and chicken born, hatched, or thrown out by folks who think country folk are anxious for their pets. He seems to roam the countryside bringing in more. Once it was a sway-backed, rheumy-eyed old horse. Tim saw the dead-wagon man loading this horse to take it to the fertilizer or glue factory in Jackson, and for fifty cents the horse became his. He tended the nag until it became frisky enough to kick up its heels and then fall and break its leg; then it was the "dead wagon" for sure. To this good day Tim won't use bought glue (he cooks up a mess of flour, water, and salt), because he is afraid he will get a bottle of glue made from his first horse.

Even when it comes to selling the pigs he raises, he puts the prospective buyer through a questioning. "Did you make plenty of corn? Are you planning to feed this little fellow twice a day? Do you give your pigs clabber?" We have to watch the corn crib, because Tim will sit and feed chickens and pigs until the corn almost runs from their ears. His argument: "They won't eat when they quit being hungry."

Off to College

T oday we took our first-born to the college of his choice. At home before we left, breakfast was wonderful—dove cooked in milk gravy, hot biscuits and muscadine jelly smelling of hot days, buzzing bees, and Waggoner Creek. The air was like wine. The whole family is filled with pride mingled with pain—pride that our son Joe is paying his way in college on a scholarship, pain that there will be a vacant chair at our table and around the fireplace.

Far to our left thunderclouds pile high, boiling black and purple. Great jags of lightning wound the clouds again and again, arousing their cries of anger and pain. Finally swift torrents of tears fall earthward, miles away. It is a sight so splendid we pull to the side of the highway and watch. Our is a ringside seat, complete with bright sunshine in a blue sky overhead.

How much of a man our son is at eighteen, solid—all 178 pounds of him—his chin blue with whiskers ready to peek through. At the college he shakes hands with his daddy, gives a gentle punch to the jaw of his brother Tim, and tumbles his sister's curls. And he gives me a kiss so sweet and tender my heart melts with love, as it did the first time I saw him, all nine pounds fighting and angry at the world, kicking the doctor who gave his backside a slap.

When I am old and my granddaughter must thread my needle and I think of days long past, dear Lord, let me remember the day our first-born went to college. ▨

Fairy Rings

H ave you seen a "fairy ring" in a nearby pasture, on your lawn, or perhaps in a city park? Spring is the time for these fairy rings to appear overnight.

When our children were small, we looked for and enjoyed these unexpected pleasures. Even when not so young, we would rush to the place where the fairy ring had been discovered, tape measure, notebooks and stubby pencils in hand, ready to measure and marvel at this seemingly magic ring there for our pleasure and enjoyment.

I recall the fun and frolic we often enjoyed on such outings. We sketched pictures of the mushrooms, tilting ones as well as upright ones. We chattered and wished longingly that we had been on the spot when the fairies danced, making their ring. When the children and I danced around the fairy rings we found, I had no idea what caused the rings to grow overnight.

An article in a farm magazine suggested that the mushrooms needed to be sprayed to kill the spores growing on dead tree roots buried underground. The article seemed to sweep away all the glitter and excitement of childhood and the many walks, talks, and wonderful hours spent with our children when we too danced around the fairy rings, marking it well, for we knew that if the weather was right on a misty moist morning we could scamper to the marked place, finding a larger ring than the one we enjoyed the last time.

I remember telling the children that the reason the grass was richer and greener after the mushrooms went away was because of the happiness the fairy folk shed as they danced, a moonbeam dust stored on a distant star where fairies lived. Before coming to earth to dance, each fairy dusted itself, especially the golden gauzy wings. Often the baby fairies would jump into the crystal vat of dust and have to be pulled out by a fond doting parent who remembered when he or she did this very thing.

To our children the way I explained the growing circle made sense and still does! You see, little fairies are growing and leaving the nursery. They are allowed the fun and fellowship of being with their elders for the dances; hence the circle had to be larger to accommodate the fairy children.

We discussed the kind of shoes the wee folk wore. To this day I can see the glittering moonray slippers, slender to the point of being toothpick narrow, gently curved on each end with tiny gold bells thereon, tinkling so softly human ears couldn't hear them. I recall Tim and Joe crawling around looking for a lost slipper. They promised it to me, faces glowing, hearts filled with love for their mother, wanting to share with her the delightful anticipation of a wee slipper for her this-and-that-shelf.

This morning when I visited with the early dawn, there for my pleasure was a fairy ring, quite large; all the fairy babies came with their elders to trip their favorite steps to the music of distant stars, in light provided by soft-as-cotton-wool moonbeams.

I am sure if our grown children had been here I would have called them to "come see." They would have been awed and not once questioned me with, "Meme, do you really believe fairies were here last night? A woman of your age, how can you believe such?"

However, the children have a young-at-heart mother, willing and eager to believe the world is good, people are wonderful, and someday when it rains it will be pure soup.

Of course I believe the fairies danced on Shady Rest last night; I happened not to see them. 🀄

Remedy for
a Wobbly Day

D o you have wobbly days? Yesterday was a wobbly day for me.
Snails had made pearl paths across the lawn and nibbled the
border of marigolds to mere strings, my nails were rimmed with
green from preparing garden sass, and I found that our laying hens
have pip and wart head. In my eternal digging of the flower beds
I turned up a nest of little animal skulls, white as ant eggs. I spent
time brooding over why anyone would bury only little skulls.

Gnat balls, large fluffy cotton white with pink dots, are growing
on the newly planted oak trees. Devil snuff boxes grow toady and
heavy-looking on a favorite fern log. Saw briars reached out to give
me deep scratches as I picked the last sweet blackberries to make
a measure of berry acid, and red bugs feasted off my fat self. I firmly
believe some people are hag-ridden and have these wobbly days once
in a blue moon. (But when good days come, aren't they wonderful?)

Last night after a wobbly day, when I simply could not sleep after
midnight, I decided to take one of my night walks. I took Dale's
old blue shirt to ward off the early morning chill and went along
the deeply rutted path to Agnes Branch. The path sides grow thick
with smut grass making convict stripes on my bare legs. Whip-poor-
wills cooed their golden brown spears of liquid sound from all sides,
so plainly clear and near I felt the urge to dodge the sounds. It
behooved me to watch my steps once I entered the woods, for whip-
poor-will nests were everywhere, spilling eggs with carelessness.

When I reached the branch, how good the thick silver bridge
boards felt, still warm from yesterday's sun. This bridge has given
trouble as long as I can remember. Once there was a ford (well rocked
and only knee deep on the tallest mule) for buggies, horseback riders,
and wagons pulled by mule or oxen. I remember old folks telling
of how those who crossed would ford the water, allowing the stock
to slake their thirst. The travellers would eat their lunch in the shade
of drooping willows; so lovely were the willows, they were often
likened to women admiring their flowing tresses in the deep pool
above the ford. In my time this bridge washed away each spring
when heavy rains flooded the countryside. The bridge would be
found and dragged back, put in place, and then nailed with heavy
spikes to wooden runners across the branch.

I found a place to sit and dangle my feet in the water. It was not gushing water, but water that spoke to sheep over a mile away, water that rejoiced over the number of quail in covey coming to drink and preen, a branch that afforded nesting places for fat red-bellies. It welcomed tadpole eggs in long strings in its side stills.

This water, now calm, had battered itself against sycamore roots as it rushed through a narrow channel above the highway to the north. Agnes Branch is a living stream, a singer of songs as it babbles over rocks in shallows. It sings of snails nibbling on leaning ferns, of nesting birds, and creeping tom cats. It sings of set hooks for mud cats, fine fellows that cook out crisp and tasty.

I listened closely to the singing, learning that muscadines are greening on ages-old vines near the sunken fence and paw-paws are well fruited near the outcropping of sandrocks. It told of buckeye bushes bearing nuts to spare for what ails a-body. It murmured that beech mast burrs are tightly closed and still growing. Chinqapins are turning shiny black though the kernels are not fully developed.

Bubbles form on my feet as they are soothed by the water. Little darting fish no larger than the merest dream come to eat the bubbles—bubble after bubble, until their tiny stomachs are puffed. Their mamas pat them with gentle fins saying, "Burp wee one, burp the silver bubbles; come away—we have fanned your soft white sand bed." I see the mama fish hover over their broods in the leafy brown shadows dappled with moonbeams. A kingfisher leaves his lonely perch, swooping toward the big waters of Waggoner Creek where he will gather his fishy breakfast.

I am reminded daylight is just over the pine forest. As I skirt the woods toward home, I notice an ages-old dead tree, so old all limbs are gone, and it now boasts only snags, fangs, and limb stubs—resting places for buzzards. How weird the tree looks, silver-gold in the low moonlight, hung with strange fruits. Huddled grey-black buzzards rustle their feathers and make clicking noises with their hooked beaks as they get ready to flock out for soaring and searching.

I have a good feeling about today: it is going to be perfect. When I reach the pasture gap, our milk cow is waiting with heavy udder. At the house the bird dogs are begging to be let out for a run. I hunger for thick sweet cream, hot sour biscuits, and blackberry jam made yesterday. Such delicious eating is usually a no-no; here in my semi-middle age every gained ounce follows a pattern laid down, perhaps thousands of years ago, which says, "Women in this fami-

ly will be wide of hip in their youth, wider and wider in old age.''
(I have seen this come true in almost every female on my father's
side of the family.) But that isn't going to bother me. Today is a
new day, and it will not be a wobbly one.

Clearing a Field

H ere in the cold of December, I remember how it was when
a new ground was being made ready for planting. A man must
have his heart in the clearing of such a field; if he doesn't, too many
stumps will have to be plowed around.

Felling the trees and dragging them into piles seems like play when
you are watching from the vantage point of a top rail of the fence
around the field. It takes both brain and brawn to get the tree piles
just so, and days to burn those piles when the wind is blowing from
the north. Several of the biggest of the mighty stumps give up the
ghost, blasted from the earth by dynamite.

Give an ordinary country man, red-necked though he may be,
a double team of horses and a new plow, then watch as he plows
rows so neat that pictures look puny beside them. Then and only
then is he a king among farm men.

When the husband and father goes out in the early dawn to hitch
Prince and Pride to the slide to haul the plow to the upper field,
he will hop on Pride for a free ride. The mother will hand him a
snack—bacon and biscuit wrapped in a clean napkin—and a jug of
fresh well water. He rides into a now-rosy dawn, back straight, stoop
of worry gone from his shoulders for a time at least.

The mother turns from the barnyard to rouse her children and
ready them for the school truck. There are two buckets of fresh
milk to strain into big stone crocks, grits to stir, bacon to crisp,
biscuits to bake, and fruit to slice. Breakfast is eaten and teeth are
brushed. The school bus honks, and the sons leave for a full day
at Liberty School.

Morning chores are soon done. The chickens are fed; these fryers
will be sold for Christmas money. Drat the little pig, he has pushed

the lower slat off his pen. The mother has to hunt the hammer—alas, it is in the tree house ten feet above the ground. A sadiron will do for nailing. She entices the pig to his pen with knocks on an empty bucket, pours soured wheat shorts into his trough, chops up collards for the laying hens, and brings in an armload of slender sticks of wood for making a quick fire when supper time comes.

The house is in fair order; beds are smoothed out, the middle of the floor is swept, milk buckets and dishes washed.

A noon meal is put together: ham and biscuits, boiled eggs, syrup cookies, and a container of coffee to be heated over a little fire the father will build at noon. A bottle of milk for baby daughter, Rose, Jr., is packed.

The mother decides to take the donkey and ties a quilt behind the saddle for naps after lunch. The little girl is delighted to ride, even though her feet come nowhere near the stirrups.

The overgrown road leads to Agnes Branch, where if one is very quiet a covey of quail can be seen taking a dust bath. Beside a shallow stretch of water, mother and child stop to watch a plate-size snapping turtle taking a snooze in the weak December sun. The child is told about the time such a turtle snapped onto the big toe of Plez Harris and would not turn loose, it was said, until it thundered.

The mother steps across a ditch, kneels beside a fallen log, and brushes aside leaves to see violets, blooming pure white on long trembling stems. It has been like this for many years—these early flowers ready and waiting when spirits need assurance that spring is on the way, that winter winds no longer will blow keen and sharp.

The big bell at the Budd household rings. Mother and child hurry over the little rise where the father is plowing. Prince and Pride pull the heavy plow through the rich land. Rows are straight, turned with sure knowledge.

The father stops the team, unhitches the horses, and turns to see his wife and daughter nearing. His face breaks into a smile. He is glad he will not have the long walk to the house for the noon meal, as no man in his right mind would ride a tired horse. The horses graze as the family eats.

The father talks of blue-ribbon pumpkins growing around a stump left for that purpose, of sweet corn to sell and can. Of course the family will eat of the delicious ears, dripping with fresh churned butter. There will be enough to dry for milling; grits, hominy, and meal will be stored for next winter's eating.

These are dreams talked about on a December day back in 1949, as I remember it and as my record book tells of the weather. The new ground did well and our sons did win blue ribbons for the pumpkins raised there. 🔳

Syrup-Making Day

I was on my way to the syrup mill. Never had the sun been more beautiful as it fell, faintly warm, on my face. A dusting of frost decorated fallen leaves and gave a sugar icing look to pale red broomstraw swaying in an early morning breeze.

A tunnel road ran through a small grove of trees. A few leaves of earthy fall colors—creamy brown, vivid red, dark purple, and bronze—made patterns of shadow and light in the powdery dust of the twisty path-road. From far away came the sound of wild geese; the air throbbed with their plaintive calls. As I lifted my eyes to search for them, they flew directly overhead, making and then breaking a perfect *V* as they winged their way southward toward food and winter shelter.

I heard shouts of laughter from the big road and hurried to hail a cane-loaded wagon for a ride. It was a wagon that had been coming to Shady Rest for many years. Uncle Pole Caston is the owner of the mill and chief cooker of the syrup.

He is very aged and cannot stand up to skim the cooking juice or oversee the grinding of the cane with the heavy steel grinders that go around and around never getting anywhere. He has taught his son the skill and lore of making good cane syrup. The son is only sixty-four and isn't trusted to see to the delicate work from start to finish. Uncle Pole comes each day to sit huddled in his padded chair.

Uncle Pole is ninety-five years old, and his eyes are dim. His teeth are store-bought and rest in his hip pocket year in and year out; in fact, he has worn out two sets carrying them in his pocket. When a child gets too close to Uncle Pole, he will reach in his pocket with a shaky hand and bring out the teeth. Before the child knows what is happening, the teeth have snapped right in his face. Often the child will cry and leave Uncle Pole alone; others are amazed and beg for more, saying, "Bite at me again."

Children who should be in school feed the grinders. A tall man totes stalks of cane from a huge pile to the grinders. Once the juice barrel is full, another person will carry dripping buckets of juice to a barrel stationed high at the upper end of the cooking pan. The flow of juice to the pan is regulated by a hand-whittled peg from a sweet gum tree limb.

Uncle Pole's son is a tall man with snow-white hair, gleaming teeth, and hands that are firm and sure on the long-handled skimmers. The skimmers are works of art made from tin that is folded to form a scoop and decorated with design holes punched with a ten-penny nail. One skimmer has a horse with long flowing mane and tail; another has a rooster with outstretched wings; another has stars and a quarter moon.

Uncle Burrel Taylor keeps the fire under the syrup-cooking pan roaring from the beginning to the end of the day. He has a long iron rake to adjust the flaming pine knots from front to back. This is done under orders from Uncle Pole.

When a cooking of syrup seems to be ready, a few drops are dripped on a syrup can lid and then taken to Uncle Pole, who dips his gnarled forefinger in the syrup, licks it with his pink tongue, closes his almost sightless eyes, smacks his lips and says, "Son, this 'lasses does fair. With age you will learn. I believe the fire needed to be hotter, so cook the next batch a mite faster. Tell Goldie to wash the strainer cloth. I can taste baggus a bit."

Uncle Pole instructs John Gooden to take the toll from this batch and put it in the shade of the firewood pile where it will not get mixed in with other toll. He expresses a fear that one can with this off-taste (only to him) might ruin his business.

A whole day can be spent at the mill. People come and go. Some drink juice and chew stalk cane, while others visit and watch the mules going around and around making the grinders turn. They yearn for childhood days when they ran barefooted up and down the baggus piles, then turned tumble-sets down to the ground on their last run up the ever-growing pile. They recall when sweet potatoes, baked in a pile of hot coals from the maw of the fire under the cooking pan, were fit for a king.

They recall skim-beer and how bumblebees flew drunk and giddy. One tells of a flock of sheep drinking soured skim, how they staggered and danced in the moonlight, and how the whole family dressed and went to the pasture to watch the sheep skip and trip about.

Night is only three fields and a hill away. I hurry home to my family knowing there will be a lamp in the window to guide me past the red clay bank. 🈳

A Letter
from a Reader

A letter from an eighty-four-year-old woman told of her sympathy for couples who are losing their farms here in the present day due to poor crops and high expenses. She wrote of the heartbreak and helpless feeling she and her husband endured when they were "put in the road" after they were unable to make the yearly thirty-dollar payment due one April to the landowner who lived in another state.

"When the letter came telling us to be gone by a certain date, we had nowhere to go. Being of the class of people some called 'poor white trash,' it wasn't easy to find another place to live, as we would be working on shares or halvers, as those arrangements were called over sixty-five years ago.

"We left the forty acres we had hoped to call our own—a good little place with a nice branch running at the back side, a pasture large enough to keep a milk cow given us as our only wedding present when we married, and a spavined red mule loaned to us by my father. The three-room house was weather-tight with a stickmoss and mud-daube chimney. I kept the house clean. How the pine floors pleased me when I scrubbed them with lye soap and creek bank sand.

"Early one morning we moved, using the slide pulled by the mule to haul our feather bed, black iron wash pot, and enough corn to feed the mule while we were on the road looking for another place to stay. Our son was two years old; we made a little nest for him in the wash pot and he rode in comfort.

"Walking along the woods road would have been pleasant if our hearts hadn't been so heavy and our shoes worn out. At eating time (we told time by the sun as we had no clock or watch—no one in either of our families had ever owned a timepiece), we stopped beside a small branch to rest and feed the mule. My husband ate part of his corn pone and wondered if we would find a place before dark. He hoped it would be close enough for him to return the next day to our lost farm to get the cow and calf and the rest of our household things, which consisted of a bedstead, two handmade oak sitting chairs, a wall mirror, water bucket, skillet, several quilts, and our few clothes for the coming winter months.

"We had to spend the night in the woods as the mule pulled up lame. The next morning the mule's foot was better. We ate corn pone dipped in water; the baby was hungry but wouldn't gnaw on the pone, or nurse either, if only for comfort.

"We were lucky; after another day on the road we found a place to farm, though the house wasn't much and the fields were overgrown with weeds and bushes. Our food had played out, and the baby was still fretful.

"The man who gave us a chance was good to us, letting us use his mules and furnishing corn and cottonseed. We planted a garden with him and his sickly wife.

"In fact the couple took us in, and over the years we lived there both families benefited from our work and his equipment. The wife had been a schoolteacher, and she taught me to read and write. She also let me use her sewing machine to make clothes for the baby we brought with us and the two born on their place. I canned for her in summer, and in the fall we dried apples and pears together. She often told me I was the daughter she never had.

"What I started to tell you is about one special day when I fixed a lunch and took the current baby and his little sister to the field where my husband was pulling corn. The oldest child was now big enough to help his daddy with some of the work. He rode the slide, keeping the mule going as needed.

"Goldenrods were blooming in old fields and trees were aflame with shades of red, yellow, and purple. When we reached the field it was almost dinner time. How good the jar of stewed blackberries and the buttered biscuits tasted. We pulled sweet pears from a tree beside a tumbled-down house. For dessert there were boiled peanuts.

"We had very little in the way of earthly goods. The reason I will always remember that day is this: as we sat resting after eating, my husband, who seldom spoke of tender things to me, put his hand on my shoulder, gave it a little squeeze and said, 'If you don't know I love you, I do. You have made me a good wife.'

"He couldn't understand why I cried." 🔳

Thrashing Peas

Yesterday I undertook to thrash a bushel of dried peas, saved for no reason at all other than that the older I get, the more I hate to see things go to waste. After the first sack was thrashed I began to think up excuses to quit this sweaty, hot business, which would pay no returns, except perhaps one or two pints of seed to plant next spring. If Dale and I ate dried peas three times a day for three months, there would still be peas to spare.

How well I recall the exciting time of pea thrashing when I was a child old enough to help. The dried peas would be put in cotton picking sacks turned wrong side out, then beaten or thrashed with sticks reserved for this job only.

Back in those times of depression, poor farm families had so few possessions that people would say fiercely, "Don't you touch my thrashing stick, lard paddle, mule curry comb, scrub broom, yard broom, sand-raking brush broom, or homemade rubbing wash board." These things were seldom loaned out. Sometimes there would be fusses and no-speaking to one who dared to take any of the precious items without asking.

It would be my pleasure to go for Uncle Burrel's thrashing stick, tucked snug in a corner of the corn crib. My brother and I also had smaller sticks used to beat dried peas from the papery hulls.

Our children enjoyed this pleasing chore when they came along. They eagerly awaited a certain day when they could take down their very own thrashing sticks and whale away on a well-stuffed sack of dried peas or a prickly sack of dried butter beans. Perhaps they would help thrash black-eyed peas, clay peas, red runner, cow peas, purple hull, or lady peas.

When the peas were out of the hull, a tarpaulin would be spread on the ground under the hay loft door, and the thrashed peas would be poured from buckets or pans at the loft door to the ground. Any breeze that happened to pass by would blow the chaff away; as a rule there would be a good draw-draft from the center hall of the barn, which was open at both ends. This would give a little push to the blowing breeze to help winnow the peas or beans.

Such jobs helped our sons keep busy, happy, and filled with a sense of well-being and importance. Best of all, their grandfather, Daddy Budd, gave them a gallon of beans or peas of their very own. With generous hearts they would offer me cups of peas to cook for their dog, Mr. Bones. They soaked peas in cold water to give to their pen rabbits, and they were never able to understand why their donkey, Emma, would have no truck with the rock-hard peas.

One job Brother and I never helped in again: that of thrashing velvet beans. Imagine being covered from head to toes with a fine fuzz from the hulls, so clinging and scratchy that nothing could ease the awful itch except fresh skimmed sweet cream. Mama could never explain to her butter customers the need for sweet cream to slather on children. 🏮

The View
From the Hill

Frankly, sixty-eight is a bit old to have a yen to run to the top of the hill behind the Gene house, to see how the valley below looks in the early morning light—so early, in fact, that the sun is still poking pink fingers over the pine forest above our house.

Many years ago, however, when our oldest son was eight, we did that very thing. We held hands. He, of course, helped me along, cautioning about deep ruts and crayfish hills when we reached the pasture. We were so winded when we reached the top of the hill that we lay on our backs in the dew-wet grass and gazed into the heavens as they turned pink. Never will either of us forget the beauty of the mist below, as it slowly faded out, and the gentle halo each tree seemed to wear as the sun rose higher and higher, until all at once the dear little valley below was all gold and green with sun and pines.

At one time some years ago, I was suprised to hear our son remark, "Do you remember how wonderful and special we felt the day we outran the sun to see the valley below the Gene house?"

Such moments are precious and surely must be related to God, His beauty and wonder. If I gave our children nothing else, I am happy they can enjoy the flash of a redbird's wing, the scud of a cloud drifting across the face of the full moon, the special blooming white flowers we plant to enjoy late at night, the larger-than-hand-size moths that sometimes hover over these blooms, and the view from the hill behind the Gene house. ▓

Anticipation

We all look forward to and anticipate things and events, from the youngest child anxious for bottle or breast feeding, to the oldest person longing and yearning for someone to stop by and chat for a few minutes to listen to him or her talk.

The child in his anticipation for the food, to soon be his, makes whimpering sounds, smacks his lips, sucks his fist and often kicks in rage, filling the air with angry cries if the food isn't forth coming at once.

The old person sits quietly, daring to hope that today someone will care enough to come help fill the empty hours of the day. In anticipation he carries on long conversations, giving and taking his part of the small talk that makes life so good. Half a day can be spent in sweet expectation, remembering joys of days gone by. Relived, they are as pleasant to the thoughts as marrow from a ham bone is to the tongue.

The elderly person lives once again happy memories and believes that today the person who listens will hear his tale through, will smile and nod at the right times making a joyous, beautiful thing of time spent with him. Forgetful that time has passed, the aged person walks again in paths green and fragrant with flowers, a path trod with the firm loving hand of his mate snuggly held within his huge hand, again laughter is loving upon the lips and eyes sparkle and dance.

Unremembered time has slowly foot-by-foot and day-by-day taken life from him. The elderly person recalls when he was full of vim and a hard day of work was only a prelude to the hours spent around his fireside. He remembers small children climbing on his knees, the cold bedrooms, icy sheets and deep slumber snug under heavy handmade quilts.

Nothing was too much for him: cold, hunger, rain, snow and hot burning sun—all added up to life in big letters. Now this sitting, sitting, sitting with longing in every line of his seamed face. The droop of shoulders, even the lax limp look of the now snow white mustache that once perkily responded to wax in a little tin box and to the cunning little brush hung on a nail close by the wavy mirror. How he loved to sweep the ends into half moons, the delight of hearing Myrtle giggle when he softly kissed her neck as she pretended a pout, saying his moustache tickled.

For a minute he remembered Jane, who came into his life during his fortieth year. "Fool's hill" his folks said he was going over— the sooner the better. But it didn't take him long to realize there was nothing under that blond curled hair and those long lashes fluttering at him when she thought nobody was looking. A weak tear runs down the lined face as he remembers the sweetness of Myrtle as she said, "Hush, we will never mention this again." True to her word, it was never talked of again in all the forty years after his foolish venture that Myrtle lived as his wife.

Those footsteps coming down the hall—perhaps they would talk. Nobody but the nurse with his dinner of soft foods—mush, eggs, custard, creamed potatoes, milk and coffee. His shrunken gums chomped together trying to get out a few words before the tray was put down and the nurse left. "Now, young lady, with all that slop for me, you should have seen the meals my Myrtle prepared for me: steaks, chicken, rabbit, hog meat, and fried potatoes."

The nurse gently but firmly said, "Now be still so I can tie this napkin around your neck, Grandpa. You eat your dinner and then I'll tucky-you in for a nice long nap." 🦋

An Unforgettable Easter

I n April 1946 the Easter rabbit left colored eggs in the front yard at our house. Both sons were under the weather (Joe with a broken leg and Tim with fever, which turned out to be red measles), so Dale and I followed the children's directions and hunted the eggs for them as they sat on the front porch.

As we ate the Easter eggs for breakfast along with grits, butter, ham, hot biscuits, and hot cocoa, we had no idea that our lives would have a drastic change within a few hours.

Mama had invited us to eat dinner with her and Daddy. Miss Bessie Lea would come home with Mama and my brother from church over Liberty way.

We were not going to church due to the chore of going to the lower pasture near the Old Lake to look for two cows expecting calves. This was Dale's time to check the cows, and if there were babies, drive them along with their mothers to the barn.

When Dale started down the road to the pasture, he met Carrie Gooden stepping along with her Sunday shoes in one hand and a chicken pie tied up in a cloth in the other. She was on her way to church about two miles beyond where the Enterprise road crossed the highway. Dale asked about Adeline, who was feeling "poly" the last few days. Carrie said she had fed Adeline and left her in bed, smoking her pipe. She said she would appreciate it if Dale would look in on the old lady when he was looking for the baby calves.

Dale had been gone about two hours when I became worried about him. I put Tim in the bed with Joe and placed the fire screen in front of the low-burning fire in the fireplace. I gave the boys strict orders to stay in bed no matter what unless the house caught on fire. I never dreamed I would soon be involved with one of the most awful house fires in our part of the country.

I cut across the sheep pasture on my way to the Old Lake, hoping to find Dale driving mama cows and their offspring to the barn. Hearing a roar, I looked toward Adeline Walker's house where she lived with Carrie Gooden. Flames were reaching toward the sky, and the smell of heart pine was strong on the slight breeze blowing from the flames toward me.

When I reached the house, I saw that it had fallen in. I could hear moaning and praying coming from a hay field beside the wire fence to the pasture. When I reached Dale and Adeline my heart turned over with pain for my husband. His hair and eyelashes were burned off; his face and hands were solid blisters. He was unable to see. He wanted me to check on Adeline, who was sitting propped against a fence post still smoking her clay pipe.

I went for help to get Dale to the house and take Adeline to Bennie Jackson's house. When I got to Mama's, she was putting Easter dinner on the table. Dale wouldn't leave Adeline until someone came for her. Daddy rang the big dinner bell for folks across Waggoner Creek to come help. I led Dale to the house, and Daddy carried him to Liberty to the little hospital run by Dr. Anderson Butler, where he was treated and sent home with instructions to return the next day for more treatment.

Within a few days we found out just what had happened down in the pasture. Dale had heard the roar of flames coming from the three-room house made from pine logs. When he reached the house the front was blazing with flames going through the roof. He called to Adeline asking her to come open the back door so he could get her out of the house. She kept saying it was getting hot in her room, and that her feet and legs hurt so bad she couldn't walk. The back door was made of heavy thick boards and was fastened with a chain run through a hole in the door and a hole bored through a log and locked in place with a heavy lock.

Dale with brute strength began kicking at the hinges to the door, finally getting the door open that way when the hinges parted from the wall. He went in the house to the room where Adeline was in her bed still complaining that she was too hot and dragged her almost-300 pounds out of the bed. Then crawling backward, he dragged her through two rooms with flames over their heads. Just as he got to the back door, the ceiling in the kitchen fell in, causing a swoosh of flame to engulf him. He rolled Adeline to the fence and into the pasture where he leaned her against a fence post. Unable to see how to get to the house, he waited, hoping someone would come for him and Adeline.

His face and head along with hands and arms swelled so badly the children were afraid of him. He would sit and suffer until it was time for more pain medicine. Each day we went to the hospital to have the dressings changed.

Dale was unable to work for over eighteen months. We took

twenty dollars each month from our small checking account at the bank, giving two of the dollars to the church as a tithe. How did we live? We had no light, water, or gas bill to pay, paid no rent and bought no clothes. My parents helped us with farm produce. We had chickens, a cow to milk, and a garden made with help from tenants on my father's place. We had a battery radio and plenty of books to read that were mailed to us from Jackson from the state library system. Dr. Butler waited for two years for his pay, which amounted to just over thirty dollars.

Miss Bessie Lea wrote to the Carnegie Hero Fund Commission, telling them about Dale risking his life to save Adeline Walker from burning to death. In July 1946 a man from the foundation came to visit Dale and the place where he nearly lost his life. We enjoyed the visit, which lasted two full days.

In November 1946 the following letter came to Dale:

> Carnegie Hero Fund Foundation
> Oliver Building
> Pittsburgh, Pa.

> My Dear Sir:
> Your letter of November 9 accepting the award made to you by the Commission has been received, and the medal will be forwarded when it has been received from the manufacturers.
> Our object in making a pecuniary award in your case was to give you the opportunity of bettering your condition in a *permanent* way, primarily to aid you to purchase a home. It is against our policy to permit an award of this kind to be used for current living expenses or for purely investment purposes, such as the purchase of stocks, bonds, mortgages, etc. And the money will not be sent to you to be placed on deposit in a bank, because it is not payable until it is needed for a particular purpose that first has been approved by us.
> When you wish to submit a definite proposition to use the pecuniary award toward the purchase of a home, please inform us, and we shall send you forms to use to give us the detailed information desired; but you should not obligate yourself, anticipating the use of the money

for any purpose, until you have been advised that your plans have been approved.

Yours very truly,
C. B. Ebersol, Manager

In January 1947 the following letter came to my husband from the Carnegie Hero Fund Commission:

Dear Sir:

Referring to your letter of November 9, accepting the medal awarded to you by the Commission in your case: I have the pleasure in informing you that the medal will be forwarded to you at the above address tomorrow by registered mail. Delivery will be restricted to you personally; and you should, therefore, arrange to receive the package and sign the registry receipt yourself. Will you please acknowledge receipt by letter, also, using the enclosed envelope.

Yours very truly,
C. B. Ebersol, Manager

Some years later when my father sold Shady Rest, and we needed a place to move to, the foundation sent the check promised. We bought the place where we now live on Highway 24, west of McComb, Mississippi. ▧

My Mother's
Death

Three sisters gathered around the bed of their mother, knowing in their hearts her time on this earth was very short. The doctor comforted them with assurance that there was no pain.

As one, the sisters became as children again, remembering the time of their childhood and a mother who had been firm with kindness, leading by example, never raising a hand to switch fat legs when naughty acts were done. Her firmest punishment was to place a child in the kitchen corner beside the piesafe, where he or she was given dish towels to fold, peas to shell, or a cake batter bowl to lick. (We were given one or two doses of "peach tree tea"—a switching with a peach tree limb—over things like sassy talk to our elders and unkindness to pets; the memory of that tea lasted a lifetime.)

Around eleven o'clock two of the sisters went home, after fond farewells to the mother who had not known anything for the past two days. One sister and the hired person took over the watching hours.

The weather was warm and beautiful, with soft scudding clouds; curtains were pushed back, the better to enjoy the nighttime, which was tempered with shadows cast from trees. A soft glow came from the night-light.

The aged mother became restless, making small, low clicking moans. She spoke, "Mama, Mama," then became still, never to move again. Her breathing was very shallow; she seemed to be holding on to life for a reason. Shortly after midnight on my mother's ninety-eighth birthday, January 2, 1989, she passed away. She had so hoped to reach 100 years and had often mentioned it when discussions of living a long time were brought up.

After Miss Aleshia and I closed Mama's still-beautiful blue eyes, bathed her, and placed a fresh white sheet over her body and face, I called my sisters, and began to mourn. At last I truly know what I am saying when I express deep sympathy when someone's mother leaves this world.

They say when times are pressing heavy, tasks seem to take over. All at once I felt that I must sweep our patio, which I began to do after turning on the outside lights.

When half-finished with this unnecessary task, I looked to the east, there to see the morning star twinkling and a crescent moon nearby, so calm and beautiful. In the shrubs small birds were twittering. Coffee smells came from the kitchen. My private, intense mourning was almost over—no matter if tears were still wetting my cheeks! 🏮

Rose Budd's Glossary
of Old-Timey Expressions

acid—Sour clabber that has been churned.

bagasse (baggus)—The part of the sugar cane stalk left after it has been put between heavy rollers to extract the juice.

band comb—Used by girls in the 1920s to keep hair from falling in their faces when they played outdoor games or studied by lamplight, when hair would make a shadow on the book or paper.

batt—A thin layer of cotton or wool fibers placed between pieces of material, as in a quilt. The raw fiber was put on one card (see entry for **cards**) and the other drawn over it until a thin batt was made, usually about five by eight inches. The cotton was picked in the fields and the seeds removed by children or mothers in spare time. The wool was sheared from sheep and worked in the same way.

bed tick—A sack affair made from ticking bought in stores. A bed-sized tick was stuffed with frazzled shucks, hay, or even dried leaves. Feather beds were made with feathers from chickens, ducks, and geese. My mother had two feather beds made with breast feathers from quail killed by my father on hunting trips. Our pillows were also made with quail breast feathers.

blue hole—Deep holes in Waggoner Creek where fishing and swimming places looked blue when early morning and afternoon sun shown on them. Most blue holes had willow trees growing on both sides of the creek.

branch—A small stream fed by underground springs or run-off from high farm land. Some are streams branched off from creeks or rivers; a wet weather branch is one that runs only after a heavy rain. Small ferns and green moss begin to grow within a matter of a few hours after a rain. This is a perfect place for children to play, as there are wide shallows only about ankle deep.

boley-holey biscuit—Biscuits prized by children anxious to get outside to play. Take one large flour biscuit, turn on edge, take the forefinger and bore a hole almost to the other side of the biscuit, put a dab of butter deep in the hole and finish filling with molasses. Squish gently so the syrup eases through the crumb inside the biscuit.

butter prints—Molded butter with pictures of animals, flowers, or writing on the top of the butter as it rests in the dish. Prints were usually made with a wooden mold in one-half pound and pound prints; my mother had five molds and Grandmother Budd had seven. Butter customers had their favorite pictures or letters, and Mama and Grandmother made sure each customer was happy with her weekly butter prints.

cards—A pair of hardwood brushes with wooden handles and fine metal teeth used to prepare cotton or wool fibers. One card was pulled downward while the other was pulled upward. Store-bought, these cards were almost a must for homemakers in the early 1900s. Dale and I have a pair of cards labeled "The Only Genuine Old Whittemore Patent No. 10 Cotton made by L. S. Watson & Co. Leicester, Mass." We were told they are over 100 years old.

chinquapins—Nuts from the tree of the same name. Squirrels are especially fond of these nuts, which are slightly bitter in taste and crunchy in texture. Children camping out at night will sometimes roast the nuts over a little fire. Fair-skinned children with deep brown eyes are often said to have "chinquapin eyes."

cooter shell—Shell of a terrapin, called a "cooter" by old time folks. Cooters were often caught, kept in pens near a stream of water, and fed on grass and kitchen scraps. Making cooter stew involved killing one or more terrapins, cutting the meat from the shells, and boiling it. The shell would be boiled as well, and when the shell had been removed, flour dumplings would be dropped in the boiling meat and broth. Any eggs in the cooter would be boiled and eaten with pepper sauce and corn pone. Cooter shells were used for dishes, pin holders, and feed bowls for chickens and dogs. Some cooter shells were as large as a big dinner plate.

copper worm—Used in cooling off a batch of moonshine. The copper worm would be placed in a trough of running water from a stream, and the steam from the cooker would pass through the worm and condense into drops of moonshine better known as white lightning. Often when "the law" came to destroy a still, they would take the copper worm as evidence that the still was out of operation.

conjure (conjer)—People thought a demon or an unjust spirit could be placed upon a person by someone who was born with a caul over his or her head or was a magician or sorcerer. These persons could conjure another person, causing bad luck or happenings.

devil's snuff box—A type of mushroom that grows on dead fallen trees or limbs. When ripe and dry, these round growths contain dark brown powder prized by many folks in years past for their healing power. A cut, gash, stab, or any wound where blood was flowing would soon heal when one of these devil's snuff boxes was squeezed over the wound and the powder allowed to settle. My grandmother would gather these puffballs and store them in glass jars in case of accidents. I too used these unique healers when our sons were small and were stumping toes, cutting fingers, and snagging themselves on fish hooks.

dog tick—Some types of female ticks that will bite their long teeth, which grow backward, into a person or animal and continue to grow, and becoming engorged with eggs. There may be as many as 5,000 eggs when the tick bursts; these eggs hatch and the cycle starts over again. Before the federal government made farmers and cattle ranchers dip their cattle, cows' ears often drooped down to the sides of their faces from the weight of so many ticks. Rabbits and squirrels were sometimes so filled with ticks that they were not good for table food.

doughty—Soft, pasty looking, fat. This word was used in the old days by some black people to describe white people who were much overweight and sweated a lot.

dummy line—A high ridge through the forest where a rail line had been laid so that cut timber could be hauled from the woods. Flat cars were used to take the timber to the nearest freight depot. The engine was fueled with wood from the forest. When the rails were removed, the ridge became known as the dummy line.

enameled rug—A forerunner of linoleum rugs. Enameled rugs were printed with bright colors in pretty designs and patterns on heavy pasteboard backing. Mama yearned for a green-and-yellow checked design to match the yellow dyed fertilizer sack kitchen curtains. A five-by-eight foot enameled rug cost around five dollars at the Liberty Mercantile run by our cousin Kate Terrell.

flying jennie—Country children enjoyed having a flying jennie on the school grounds. The trustee board, composed of male parents, would cut down a tall pine tree, leaving a stump about three feet tall. The stump would be whittled to a round stub about twelve inches high. The trunk of the fallen tree would have all limbs trimmed off and a hole would be bored to fit the projection on the stump, with a bit of room to spare. The stub on the stump and the hole in the tree trunk would be greased with hog fat, and pieces of boards would be nailed across the tree trunk for handholds. A child would get on each end of the tree trunk and hold on for dear life, while other children would begin pushing the tree trunk until it was flying around. If a child happened to fall off, he knew not to stand up but to crawl to safety. Only the brave and hardy enjoyed the flying jennie!

foot log—A substitute for bridges over small streams and narrow places in creeks. A farmer would cut a tree on one bank, allowing it to fall across the stream. Once the limbs were trimmed off the trunk, a nice sturdy way to cross the water was in place for many years. Best of all, cows couldn't walk across the foot log.

garden sass—In spring time when there were leaf and head lettuce, dill, radishes, tender greens, green onions, English peas, and mustard and turnip greens in the garden, Mama would send us out to gather garden sass for her noon meal. No root vegetables were called garden sass.

ground hog saw mill—A small saw mill used to clear all the timber from land that was to be farmed. A mill owner who went in without permission to clear cut would be called a ground hog.

ground spewer—Very cold weather. Wet ground would spew up in ice, banks beside roads would have spewed clumps of ice, and barnyards would have horse and cow tracks filled with spewed ribbons of ice.

high water—A game of jump rope in which the thrown rope would be held high so that the jumper had to exert herself not to touch it. If she tired, she would say "calf rope" and not be called out.

liderd knots—Pieces of fat pine found in woods, mostly in the form of knots where limbs had grown from the trunks. Liderd knots are rich in turpentine and blaze quickly when lit. During possum hunting time, hunters often carried a flaming pine knot to light the way; these knots cost nothing at a time when coal oil for lanterns was fifteen cents per gallon.

mendets—Round pieces of metal with a cork pad between, used to mend articles such as cooking pots and pans made of granite, enamel, and aluminum. Hot water bottles can also be mended with these small interesting helpers. During the depression, housewives kept a card of mendets on hand. Here in my fifty-second year of marriage and housekeeping, I know exactly how many chicken dumplings plus meat from two chickens will fill a mended pan. The tiny mendet in one corner doesn't spoil the pie.

milch cow—A cow giving milk, one kept for milking. The word was used by many farmers when speaking of their favorite cow with calf by her side; they said the word as it is spelled.

mill tail—On the banks of Waggoner Creek one of my foreparents had a cotton gin and grist mill both run by water power. There were tall heavy gates which, when closed, contained the creek water in what was called a "mill tail." Water pouring over a dam caused the machinery to run; when water wasn't needed, the gates were opened.

monument yard—A small park next door to the Presbyterian Church in Liberty. There is a marble monument listing the names of soldiers from Amite County killed in the Civil War. Cedar trees and benches made this a nice place to rest when Auntie and I made trips to the county seat.

mud cats—A slick-skinned fish similar to blue cats. Mud cats, which seldom grow over eight inches long, have a wide mouth with whiskers, are a muddy-blue color, and feed on the bottoms of small creeks and branches. These fish are a delight to children who enjoy bringing home a nice string of fish for their mama's noon meal. Fried fish, hot biscuits, brown gravy, and rice make a feast, and best of all the children can say, "We furnished the fish for dinner."

mutch—A cap worn by housekeepers to protect their hair from dust; also worn by those who want to hide kid curlers or unkempt hair. The cap is usually made from white material, and most have a ruffle around the edges for decoration. A drawstring keeps it snug over hair. These caps were worn years ago; it is said that the old women and children wore them in Scotland and France. Evidently the Scotch-Irish in our family brought this morning cap with them when they came to America.

oil sausage—These different and delicious sausages came in finger-long sections packed in oil, usually in five-gallon cans. The sausages were made from ground beef and were highly seasoned and colored with red dye. They were a special treat for country people who wanted to buy a little snack in the grocery store: sausage, crackers, a slice of cheese, and a tall ice-cold pop. Dessert would be a "stage plank," which was a flat ginger cake with vivid pink icing—two came in a paper envelope. This lunch cost twenty cents. Our uncle Welch threw in the stage planks, saying, "You all brought me your trade, now it is my treat."

opium gum—Around 1840 to 1870 opium gum could be bought in grocery stores or drug stores; it came in flattened, rather sticky, balls. Our great aunt Sallie often told me how the gum was used: a small piece would be sliced from the ball and placed between the gum and upper cheek, where it melted or dissolved. People often became addicted to this gum, especially women who had used it for pain relief during childbirth.

plunder (noun)—Lots of small things such as household necessities and equipment for animal doctoring. A semi-doctor (self-taught) carried a bag of home-grown medicine, bandages, etc., along with sharp knives, number eight sewing thread, a big-eyed needle, and other odds and ends. When K. Green came to doctor on any animal he would put down his great big bag, saying, "Now let me get out my plunder and get to doctoring."

Long ago, folks did not have much in the way of bought things in their homes—it was make do or do without. I recall homemade fly swatters, turkey wing fans, battling sticks used to beat washed and boiled clothes, graters made from tin cans nailed to a board and a dainty one made from a zinc screwtop jar lid with the porcelain liner removed. Women carried many things in their purses: sugar biscuits for the baby when it cried in church, a chamois rag to wipe sweat from a brow, a hair net, hairpins, a string of spools for the toddler to play with when the sermon went on and on. Ask any woman back in the long ago what she had in her purse, and nine times out of ten you would hear, "Nothing much—lots of plunder."

Our sons loved their plunder: homemade spinning tops, slingshots made from forked limbs, inner tube rubber for draw-backs, and an old shoe tongue for the rock holder, marbles made from red clay and vinegar, then baked in Mama's wood stove, popguns made from elderberry stems and green chinaberries to shoot in the popguns.

plunder (verb)—When homes are broken into with robbery in mind and the thieves find nothing to their taste, they often plunder the home, breaking glass from the windows, spilling drawers on the floor, dragging mattresses outside and turning the hose on them, cutting carpets to shreds, tearing curtains from the windows—even quilts hanging on the walls for decoration are ripped down. All in the name of plunder.

pore folks' tea—This kind of tea has been around for well over 100 years in our family. Natchez, where coffee and tea were bought on yearly trips, was a long way from Shady Rest, and pore folks' tea was a hot drink easy to make from ingredients that were always on hand. You take one tablespoon of sugar and one tablespoon of sweet cream, place in a cup and stir well, and add boiling water. Grate a bit of nutmeg or a small piece of cinnamon bark for extra flavor. Take outside, sip, and enjoy country living. Our relatives who came from Ireland had small rocks that were full of holes or pores; one of these little rocks would be dropped in the cup with the cream and sugar and stirred well before the water was added. The rock was saved for another making of pore folks' tea.

potato bank—A place to store sweet potatoes. You dig a hole about two feet across and one foot deep, pour in several buckets of washed rocks, and add layers of hay or oat straw. After potatoes are dug (do not wash), let them air dry under a shade tree for a day or two, then pile them on top of straw, cover with more hay or straw, and pour dry dirt over them (red clay is best) about six inches deep. Cover with boards and black tarpaper. Potatoes should not freeze in cold weather. When ready to have a mess of baked potatoes make a small opening at the top and remove as needed.

pre-salad days—From nine to teen years when the future seems far away.

raise Cain—A great commotion such as someone fussing at a child, servant, wife, or others when they can't answer back.

rap-jack—A game children played in years past in which long limber switches were used. A line was drawn in the dirt and the child who had a switch in each hand would give a dare: "Don't cross that line—if you do I'm going to rap-jack you." All raps were below the knees. Other children were standing around, hoping the two playing would tire and let the watchers have a chance. Sometimes one child would rap-jack a half dozen or more children and win the game. When a child wanted to give over and quit, he was supposed to yell "calf rope." As a rule when the rap-jacked children arrived at their homes, their parents finished their fussing with a whipping for good measure, even though parents considered it common for children to play rap-jack.

red bellies—Creek perch or sunfish; any fish with a reddish cast to the belly.

rusty (cut a rusty)—Older people as well as children can "cut a rusty." Grown people become loud, cry, moan, and throw things when they are trying to get their way. Children have fits of temper, falling to the floor sobbing, weeping, and kicking, often taking their rusty cutting to the point of holding their breath until their faces turn blue. Our sister Bess was well known for her rusty cutting and breath holding. Mama was afraid she would die. Dr. Quin assured Mama he had never heard of anyone being buried from rusty cutting.

sadirons—Heavy irons with flat, smooth bottoms and curved handles joined at the back and front. The handle became too hot to use without heavy, thick pads of cloth. These irons came in weights from two to twelve pounds. In summer an outside fire was made to heat the irons and the person doing the ironing took the ironing board outside to enjoy a cool breeze. Some families had a charcoal furnace large enough to heat three irons at a time; others used the cooking stove while preparing dinner. In winter sadirons were often heated in front of the family fireplace, so that the wife could chat with her husband while keeping an eye on the children. Wrapped in woolen cloth, a sadiron was a joy to have in bed next to cold feet or to comfort an aching back.

salad days—Our grandmother Budd often mentioned salad days in connection with tender greens and other vegetables used in salads. During my salad days I started going to play parties and wearing pretty clothes. It was a time to take on some of Mama's chores to give her a little rest and to repay her for all the things she had done for me. It was the beginning of growing up, getting ready for the time of courtship, and for having a job with my own money to spend, preparing for marriage, a home, and children.

This expression has been around at least since Shakespeare's time. In *Antony and Cleopatra,* act 1, scene v, the following words appear: "My salad days,/When I was green in judgment,..." (One aged lady told me that she had never had salad days until the last ten years, when for the first time in her life she is doing as she pleases—not one person to answer to or boss her around.)

set hooks—Hooks that are set out at night; they are baited and hung from fishing poles that are stuck in the creek banks. When the night work has been done, supper eaten, and a time spent visiting with the family, the father will say to his sons, "Let's go check our set hooks." There will likely be several eels, good-eating fish, a turtle or two, and lots of fun and fellowship. The catch is removed, the hooks rebaited and set out again. Early morning will find someone running the hooks, taking off the catch, and winding the lines and hooks on a green limb that will be brought to the house to dry on top of the smokehouse. Children are fond of set hook fishing.

shivaree—A serenade to newlyweds. Country folks made a big thing out of the shivarees they gave when a just-married couple went to their new home or to the home of one set of parents; as a rule there were more people at the shivarees than at the wedding. Noisemakers, singing, and rowdy jokes were part of the festivities. Catcalls were made to the newlyweds urging them to come out and greet the guests—at least to offer a cup of hot cider or a sip of moonshine. After a spell, the groom would have enough of this foolishness; often he would shoot a shotgun toward the sky with a promise that the next shot would be direct from the front porch.

shrub—A beverage made from fruit juices. Our shrubs are non-alcoholic.

skeeter hawks—Local name for dragonflies often seen around creeks, branches, and rivers where the water runs shallow.

skim beer—When sugar cane juice was cooked in open pans at syrup mills, a scum would rise to the top of the boiling juice and have to be removed with tin skimmers. The "skim" was put in wooden barrels and allowed to ferment until those who liked this beer said it was ready for drinking. Often homemade yeast cakes were dropped in the fermenting juice to hasten the working time of the beer. Skim beer would be drawn from the bottom of the barrels through an inserted piece of green hollow reed cane (found growing near the Old Lake) in the bung holes. When the beer was drawn off, workers drank their fill and often had to take naps on the baggus pile. It was said this beer had the kick of a wall-eyed mule.

slide—A wooden box with green oak runners nailed to the bottom. Slides were used to haul fertilizer, feed, seeds, children, and firewood in small amounts and to gather corn when harvest time came. One man could pull corn and drive the slide from one end of the row to another, thereby making it possible for other family members to do farm chores as needed. Slides were pulled by horse, mule, oxen, goat and, for short distances, men and women. Children especially loved having a slide made for them, getting a billy goat to pull it, and directing him up and down the country roads. Having their very own farm equipment on a smaller scale made them feel important.

stomp—In olden times when horse, ox, or mule power was used to pull wagons, buggies, carriages, carts, and slides, and when people rode horseback, front yards were used for hitching the animals; most families had large yards where the unhitched animals could move about. When company came the host would say, "Unhitch your stock so they can stomp about and rest." This is how the word stomp came about. On Shady Rest there was an acre front yard or stomp.

stork scissors—A small pair of scissors made in the shape of a long-legged stork, used to do dainty cutwork embroidery. The long bill of the stork made the cutting blades. Sewing kits, baskets, and boxes came with these interesting bright gold-colored scissors, along with threads of all colors, needles, tape measure, a needle threader, and a small Bible.

sugar teat—Take half of a small flour biscuit, place on a square of clean white cloth, put a lump of butter on the biscuit, cover both with a generous sprinkle of sugar, gather edges of cloth, twist together, and tie with a strip of cloth, making sure the edges stick up enough for the child to hold on to so he or she will not swallow the teat. Using your fingers, mash the whole thing until it starts oozing through the cloth. Give to one fussy crying child to suck on.

thumps—Extra heartbeats, thought by old folks to be caused by too much coffee. The person with thumps had to rest and fan until it passed. Our aunt Eula, a confirmed coffee drinker who kept the coffee pot filled the whole day, was often seen resting with a cold cloth on her forehead, recovering from thumps. Now people speak of heart palpitations.

toady—The look of a warty toad frog, with bumps and freckles.

toll—When farm folks went to the grist mill to have corn ground into meal, hominy, chicken chops, or cow feed, the mill owner would keep a portion of the corn for his pay. This was called toll. It was usually a pound of unground for twenty pounds of ground corn.

Syrup makers would take one gallon toll out of each fifteen gallons of molasses made at their mill.

tommy walkers—A pair of poles fitted with foot rests about three feet from the ground. (These are also called stilts.) As a rule, there would be a leather strap from the foot rest to the pole, leaving space for the foot. At Shady Rest tommy walkers were made from green sweet gum saplings with the limbs trimmed off. We went stalking about the yard and pastures on these poles and often had races. Taking them to school was a no-no!

velvet beans—Beans that were fed in the pods to cattle. Velvet beans were planted in the fields at the same time corn was, and the vines climbed up the corn stalks, blooming and making clusters of fuzzy pods. The velvet beans had to be pulled before the corn could be gathered; workers went through the fields of corn, picking the beans by hand and putting them in long sacks which dragged on the ground. This was an awful task, as the fuzz from the pods stung like ants. Strong men were known to leave the field, run to Waggoner Creek or Agnes Branch, jump into the water, and stay until their bodies were at ease. Milk cows were especially fond of these beans and would often break into a corn field to feast on the beans before they were dry enough to pick.

water glass eggs—Eggs that were put down for winter storage in water glass—a syrupy liquid made from dissolving sodium silicate in water. A five-gallon stone crock would be filled with infertile eggs (fertile ones would not keep) and the water glass poured over the eggs to seal the pores and preserve them.

water house—An area on the front or back porch where people could wash up. A shelf nailed between two posts about three feet from the porch floor would hold water buckets with dippers, wash bowls, or wash pans, along with soap dishes, which were often small cooter shells, one holding sweet soap and the other pine tar soap. Towels would be hung on wooden pegs on the posts, or if a roller towel was used it would be nailed to a nearby wall. Often waterhouses were latticed in to shade bathers from the morning sun. Elephant ears were usually planted at the edge of the porch by the waterhouse; the soapy water caused the plants to grow so tall they often reached the porch eaves.

One neighbor known for his odd ways would be bathing on his front porch, naked as a jay bird; if he heard a buggy or horseback rider coming he would run over and squat behind a porch rocker, much to the dismay of his long-suffering wife.